WITHDRAWN

generation T

108 ways to transform a T-shirt

megan nicolay

workman publishing / new york

▪ to everyone who finds treasure in trash ▪

Library of Congress Cataloging-in-Publication Data
Nicolay, Megan
Generation T: 108 ways to transform a t-shirt / by Megan Nicolay.
    p. cm.
ISBN-13: 978-0-7611-3785-6; ISBN-10: 0-7611-3785-8 (alk. paper)
    1. Clothing and dress—Remaking. 2. Clothing and dress—
    Alteration 3. T-shirts. I. Title.
TT550.N54 2005
        646.4'04—dc22   2005042677

Workman books are available at special discounts when purchased in
bulk for premiums and sales promotions as well as for fund-raising or
educational use. Special editions or book excerpts can also be created
to specification. For details, contact the Special Sales Director at the
address below.

Designed by Barbara Balch

Workman Publishing Company, Inc.
708 Broadway
New York, NY 10003-9555
www.workman.com

Printed in the United States of America

First printing: March 2006
10 9 8 7 6 5 4 3 2 1

acknowledgments

There are so many people who helped give this book life. First, a big rock 'n' roll shout-out to everyone who donated T-shirts. I would never have been able to undertake this without their help: Eric Brown, Kevin Cunningham, Erica Dagley, Beth and Chris Doty, Meghan Dove, Andy Eisenberg, Micah Hales, Alex Heir at *deathattack.com,* Tisola Logan, Planet Aid, Suzanne Rafer, Marcia Reynolds at Wilkesboro Elementary School, Cory Schreier, Robyn Schwartz, Nina Shen, Sarah Stacke, Kayte Terry, Al Vindito, Catherine Wong, and Lissa Ziegler. Second, a huge and humble thank-you to my roommates, who graciously put up with (for far too many months) an apartment decor that consisted of mountains of the acquired T-shirts. A sincere thanks to Alison Fassnacht and Karisa Horsley for temporary use of their T-shirt quilt, to Suzy Becker for her generosity with drawing materials and veteran advice, and to all my ladies with the Department of Craft for their enthusiasm for all things handmade.

To my dear brainstorming brigade who faithfully attended late-night Tee-for-Two Parties, helping me get the word out and the tone right. Foremost, Rebecca Schiff (who, despite labeling herself among the non-crafty, can slash a mean T-shirt), for the perfect title, for keeping me (and the book) breathing in the past year, and for simply "getting it" when it was just an idea. Whether it took hour-long phone calls from hundreds of miles away, a dash across the street, or a rendezvous in the park, thanks to Cristina Betances, Chloe Godwin, Becca Hanson, Elia Herman, Jeannette Lee, Andra Olenik, Sara Rowbottom, and Emily Weinstein for their wit and wisdom in helping me give names and personality to the projects.

To all my Tee Party people who showed up one April weekend to help finish making every project in the book (and then some), I am so grateful. Lori Barrett, Kim Cherubin, Emily DePrang, Sara High, Eunice Liu, Leda Marritz, Kim Newman, Lily Rothman, Beth Svinarich, Jessica Swain, Mary Heath Swanson, and Lily Tilton, I'll party with y'all any day of the week. And my A-listers who *really* showed up to party (we're talkin' weeks at a time!), the esteemed Lady Diana Schoenburn, Madame Michelle Bylenok, my scissor sisters Sophie and Ariana, and my dear mom—each managing, in those weeks, the cutting and stitching equivalent of spinning gold out of straw.

An eternal thank you to my family: my parents, Franz and Susan, for always allowing me (and pushing me) to express myself in any and every medium I could get my hands on, and my brother Franz and my sisters Sophie and Ariana for inspiring me always with their music, drawing, dance, and stories. Thank you to Luke for being so punk rock inside, for finding in me a good charity to dispense his virtually unmatched T-shirt donations, for rooting through garbage bags on Broadway sidewalks for supplies, and for knowing that the fastest way to this lady's heart was with a seam ripper.

Thank you to the countless, anonymous T-shirt DIYers I tracked down on the street, to the musicians who put on the shows that attract so many rebel fashion-istas, and to the store people who stock those clothing racks that help give me the impulse to do it myself.

Thank you to Peter Workman and all of the Workman crew who pitched in to make this a creative reality. To Barbara Balch for her wonderful design work; Lynn Strong for her passion for detail; Anne Cherry for her humor and care with words; Doug Wolff for keeping us on track; Katherine Camargo for helping us cross the finish line; my publicist, Sarah O'Leary, for her charm-ing and reassuring efficiency; the unflappable Kristy Ramsammy in photo research for her dedication and positive energy; Beth Hatem, who has all the poise and versatility of a superhero (I'm still trying to come up with something she can't do!); and editor in chief Suzie Bolotin for her everlasting and radiant patience. Thank you also to the photo team—what an undertaking!

Leora Kahn and Aaron Clendening for the organization; stylist Ellen Silverstein for her expertise; lensman Andrew McLeod and his henchmen Henders Haggerty and John Lansford; my lovely models, Erin Grega, Jorden Haley (*birduvprey.com*), Rashida Harris, Beth Hatem, Briana Masterson, Dré Mazzenga, Elizabeth Wong, and the delightful gentlemen from FDNY's Ladder 6; and the hair and makeup gals, Amy Lin and Melissa Crist: thank you for helping it all come together right. And I am so grateful also to the swell lot of people who have tweaked, cheer-led, retrieved lost computer files, and spread contagious enthusiasm along the way: Steve Andrews, Patrick Borelli, Anthony Cacioppo, Jarrod Dyer, Nick Caruso, Michael Fusco, Dietrich Gehring, Joe Goldschein, Ellice Goldstein, Frank Greally, Paul Hanson, Joelle Herr, Kim Hicks, Marta Jaremko, Wayne Kirn, Mari Kraske, Anne Lamb, Kathy Maloy, Justin Nisbet, Saundra Pearson, Barbara Peragine, Kristina Peterson, Helen Rosner, David Schiller, Tod Seelie, Kim Small, Leslie Stem, Janet Vicario, Carolan Workman, and Katie Workman.

Lastly, for trusting me and giving me my best challenge yet, thank you to my editor, Ruth Sullivan, who, when I brought her my idea and told her, "I could *so* write that book," suggested, "Well, maybe you should. . . ." Thank you, thank you, thank you.

contents

(back)

Top: **15** *shoulder chic, page 54*
Skirt: **51** *snip, crackle, pop!, page 133*

chapter 4: **flir-tee girls** 96

**14 tube tops (and halters, too!)—even less
shirt, even more style.**

chapter 5: **skir-tee girls** 128

**23 projects that take the T-shirt downtown—
and we're not talking about the financial
district in New York City.**

Top: **37** *bodice snipper, page 100*
Skirt: **67** *bohemian wrapsody, page 170*

chapter 6: **the t-zone** 184

From leg warmers to hats, handbags to ponchos, checkbook covers to throw pillows, 16 projects that are perfect accents for the body and the home.

chapter 7: **t-wrecks** 224

After the T-shirt deconstruction and reconstruction, here are 19 ways to "get scrappy" with the leftovers.

80 *a tee in the 'pod, page 200*

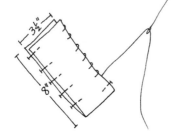

the grand finale

the brooklyn tee party: a revolution begins

y friends often tease me about my DIY obsession. Whenever I see something on a store rack I absolutely love, I'll run my hands over the item, admire the craftsmanship, and imagine the outfit it will complete. Then, upon seeing the price tag, I'll release the garment from my fingers with a sneer of incredulity—"Forty dollars?! I could *so* make that."

What can I say? I'm cheap. (Though I prefer "thrifty," "bargain-hunter," or "penny-wise.") I don't like spending a lot of money, and I don't like other people

The Tee Squad: taking tee fashion to the streets

spending a lot of money, either. And yet I love fashion, one of the most high-priced hobbies out there. So how, you may ask, do I indulge my desire for fashion-forward designs? Simple: I do it myself.

More than saving money, I love making things. I like to be able to take a step back from an outfit I've doctored and feel the proud satisfaction that comes from knowing, "Hey, I *made* that." It's an even better feeling than having your artwork on a wall (or refrigerator!)— you get to wear it.

The T-shirt has always been romanticized as a blank canvas. With its rich history of messaging (from commercial logos to school and team allegiances to social and political expression), it is especially appropriate to DIY. I started early. When I was in sixth grade, my four best friends and I staged a protest against the Gulf War. We used permanent markers to decorate old Hanes T-shirts with peace signs and slogans lifted from our parents' generation ("bread not bombs" and "make love, not war") and assembled during recess, marching past the foursquare courts and seesaws. Quite the little radicals. Twelve years later, I found myself marching down Broadway in New York (with a considerably larger crowd), rallying for peace in Iraq, wearing a T-shirt emblazoned with my new political agenda, reflecting a new message of hope.

We all have memories like these—and we more than likely have a T-shirt in our dresser to commemorate every one (the state basketball championship, the rock concert at Coney Island, the family reunion in Las Vegas . . .). But the tee does more than make us feel nostalgic. As universal as jeans, T-shirts have proven themselves in the world of fashion with their unparalleled comfort, versatility, and longevity. We sleep in them, play sports in them, party in them, rock out in them. Paired with jeans, a skirt, or those tight leather pants, the tee is a classic—it will never go out of style. It's James Dean, Marlon Brando, Bruce Springsteen. It's Sid Vicious. It's Christy Turlington, Drew Barrymore, Angelina Jolie. It's Bart Simpson. It's Debbie Harry, Joan Jett, Chrissie Hynde. Now it's yours—to reinvent.

I've been refashioning T-shirts for more than half my life. For years it's been a way to express myself—my sentiments, my style—on a small budget. These days I refashion with scissors. Think about it, what other crafty trend lets you prick, rip, cut, and slash? It's an amazing release of aggression. (Especially if the old T-shirt you're tackling belongs to an ex . . . hey, easy with the scissors.) But this type of refashioning isn't new. Girls and guys have been taking scissors to their tees since Jennifer Beals cut the necks out of her shirts in *Flashdance* or the two Coreys readied for school in *Dream a Little Dream.*

There are still groups of punk kids and art students who cut and slash their way to self-made fashion, but the DIY *style* has gone mainstream, only without the actual DIY. Boutiques and department stores, both high end and low, are selling clothes with the rough-edged, unfinished, I-made-it-myself look. And that's where you come in, putting the "You" back into Do-It-Yourself.

A Tee Grows in Brooklyn:
The author and her sister Sophie make
"Heavy Meshinery."

You are a generation of hip, resourceful, creative DIY warriors: Bored by the traditional T-shirt, you want something with personalized pizzazz. You want to "waste not, want not." You like clothes but don't want to be retail clones or slaves to commercial logos or fashion mags. Descendants of the punk movement, you still know the appeal of a well-placed safety pin.

So gather up those countless old T-shirts won at sporting events, collected at credit card sign-ups, promotional giveaways, or the random thrift store (even when they didn't quite fit), and forget about saving them for a special occasion (that, by the way, is never going to happen). I know you're sentimentally attached to some of those rags, but why not turn them into something you'll actually wear?

Enter *Generation T*. Pick a style and go with it. And if one project's not your cup of "tee," flip a few pages more. There are plenty of styles to choose from—punked-out tees, saucy tanks, flirty skirts, funky bikinis. Accessorize with leg warmers, headbands, and hand-bags, or furnish your room with throw pillows, rugs, and blankets. Not feeling so crafty? Not a problem. Even if you count yourself among the craft-illiterate—you couldn't care less about homemade potpourri and shudder at the sight of origami—you'll find something to inspire you in *Generation T*. You don't have to learn a new skill (a third of the projects are no-sew). You don't have to shop for materials at specialty stores (forget the hand-spun angora yarn). For easy use, each project is rated 1 to 5 for level of difficulty. But you needn't be scared off by those 5s—even the projects that do require a needle and thread can be made entirely by hand.

Whether you're an old pro or just a beginner, think beyond these pages. Add your own personal signature to the projects. Sketch your ideas or embellishments on the blank T-shirt outlines at the back of the book (page 254). Then grab your scissors and the nearest T-shirt and repeat after me, "I could *so* make that."

And you don't have to do it alone. My personal response to outrageously high-priced DIY-style fashion was to host a Brooklyn Tee Party, but instead of tossing outworn tees overboard, we rescued them. Everyone

A Tee Party: Chloe and Sara get down and dirty with needle and thread.

brought a bag of old T-shirts—a mix of golden oldies and throwaways—to cut up and refashion. We exchanged ideas over glasses of iced tea and spirits, and snipped and quipped late into the night. We shared stories of our old T-shirts and toasted their new beginnings.

These Tee Parties are not exclusive to Brooklyn. They can be held in living rooms and dorm rooms across the country, over kitchen counters or picnic tables, in the hippest of Home Ec classes and summer camps. So brandish your scissors—join the party. Before you retire that saggy, baggy old tee, restyle it. Resuscitate it. Reclaim it.

"The wonder of a T-shirt is that
it's all about what you bring to it.
The plain white cotton is a blank
canvas for your individual stamp."

--designer Charles Nolan

ready, set, sew

The no-nonsense no-holds-barred guide to getting the party started— all the materials, stitches, and insider techniques for T-shirt transformation.

Let's get a few things straight. Getting crafty with *Generation T* does not mean adding glitter to every accessory. It does not mean "BeDazzling" everything from your calculator to your toothbrush or affixing pre-tied bows to your blazer. No adhesives (that includes hot glue guns). No puffy paint. You need scissors, needle and thread, safety pins, and sheer moxie.

Generation T is all-inclusive—if you wear T-shirts, you're part of it. If you own a pair of scissors, you're already equipped to make one-third of the projects in this book. The others that do require a needle and thread can be made entirely by hand, no sewing machine needed—though some projects will go a lot faster if you use one.

But before you slash, read this chapter. "Tee Off!" is your reference; it includes the materials and the basic stitches and sewing techniques you'll need to make all the projects in the book. Refer back to it whenever you hit the proverbial snag or need a quick refresher course.

finding inspiration

Beyond the 108 projects and 175 variations offered here, you can find inspiration for DIY fashion everywhere. From an item on a store hanger, a friend's closet, or the outfit of a complete stranger walking down the street (just don't shadow the person for more than a block). Grab a piece of paper, a napkin, a receipt—whatever's handy—and sketch it out to try later at home.

If you see something you like in a magazine or catalog, tear out the picture and copy the design.

Chances are you can make it—or something better. Observe the world around you. I keep my sketch pad handy and scribble down design notes about outfits I see people wearing on the subway platform, on the crosswalk, at an outdoor café. At a punk rock show I snapped pictures of fans backstage.

Some of my designs come into my head in very abstract ways—a shape inspires me here, a color catches my eye there, and then the two meet. Let yourself be inspired by your surroundings. I was sitting in Washington Square Park one summer afternoon, eating my lunch and sketching pictures of the arch under construction. Several of those sketches, combined with some from my daily street fashion observations, inspired the Cover Girl halter top design in Chapter 4. The lesson here is: Keep your eyes peeled, and your sketch pad handy.

gathering supplies

Each project in *Generation T* is written like a recipe, starting with a list of ingredients (a.k.a. materials and supplies) and followed by the steps needed to create it. Basic ingredients include a T-shirt (bare minimum), scissors (almost always), needle and thread, straight pins, chalk, and a ruler.

T-Shirts You'll need one or two T-shirts for most of the projects here. So where can you find them? My largest collection includes old softball uniforms, from Little League tees (a very hot commodity on the thrift store circuit) all the way up to high school

My love affair with T-shirts cannot be separated from my love affair with the jersey fabric from which they are made—my affection spans both emotional and practical realms (T-shirts are comforting *and* comfortable). Besides being one of the most accommodating fabrics out there, jersey is especially amenable to being cut up and refashioned. A little insight into my relationship:

1. Jersey doesn't unravel or fray, so you can leave your cuts raw and unfinished for that rough-edged look.

2. It's incredibly low-maintenance—it doesn't require ironing and demands less upkeep and care than most other fabrics.

3. It's easy to sew and fit, and drapes well.

4. It tends to curl at the ends when you cut it—which is especially handy when cutting drawstrings.

5. Did I mention it's just plain fun to wear? But you already knew that.

summer softball tees. If you don't have quite the stock-pile that I have, fear not. T-shirts are everywhere. Scout around for promotional giveaways (good sources for clever slogans or, at the very least, exciting splashes of color) and credit card sign-ups (you can always cancel them). Root around in your own bottom drawers for bar mitzvah tees, travel souvenirs, and rock concert treasures. You can even rescue one of your dad's old T-shirts before it's reduced to a household cleaning rag (never thought you'd be raiding Dad's closet, did you?). You'd be surprised at how many free tee opportunities there are out there. (If you opt for the thrift-store purchase, just make sure you wash the tee before you start slashing it.)

When you're choosing a T-shirt to refashion, pay attention to the weight of the fabric, as well as its stretch and color. The weight depends on the material

tee trivia

Stretch It Out: In the 1980s, DuPont de Nemours chemists developed Lycra®, which allowed the T-shirt to cling to the body without restricting movement.

(is it 100% cotton? a 50/50 blend?). T-shirts made from blended fabrics are slightly lighter than all-cotton ones and will drape more elegantly (they're also more susceptible to static cling). Despite being heavier, all-cotton fabric is more breathable—which is why we wear it on the hottest summer days. You can make any project out of just about any T-shirt, but keep in mind what you want the final outcome to look like and use your common sense. If a shirt is stiff and rigid to begin with, it's not going to make the flounciest skirt. And the super-soft lived-in T-shirt will never regain its shape, so don't expect a structured A-line skirt out of that one.

On to the subject of stretch. The beauty of jersey knit is that it stretches a little in every direction. Single-knit jersey stretches from 20% to 25% across the grain (that's horizontally across a T-shirt). Check out the stretch scale below. You can measure any piece of fabric against this scale to test its capacity for stretch. When spandex or other artificial materials are added to the mix, jersey can stretch more than 35% (and it retains its shape better).

choosing between right and wrong

When I refer to the "right" and "wrong" sides of the fabric, I'm not expressing moral judgment. On a T-shirt, the "right" side is the outside of the shirt; the "wrong" side is the inside. And jersey knit is actually visibly different on each side—there are flat vertical ribs on the right side and dominant horizontal lines on the wrong side. The right side of the fabric (the outside of the T-shirt) is meant to be seen; the wrong side (inside) is a little softer against your skin.

Note: If a jersey fabric is double knit (specialty fabric that is double-thickness) right and wrong sides will be nearly indistinguishable.

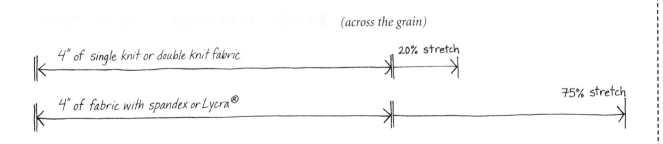

(across the grain)

4" of single knit or double knit fabric — 20% stretch

4" of fabric with spandex or Lycra® — 75% stretch

I like to try on the T-shirt I'm using before I start a project—even if I'm making a skirt—to see how it stretches and hangs. It's important to be aware of the original fit of the T-shirt (the fabric will hug the same way whether it's across your bust or your butt). For instance, if your shirt has 3% spandex and is a little snug around your shoulders and torso, cut off the sleeves and make it into one of the fitted tank tops—you avoid the tight shoulders and accentuate the tight torso.

And lastly, color. Feeling timid about picking your color palette? Here's an exercise: Throw all your T-shirts in a pile on the floor and look for colors and patterns that work well together (match complementary colors and mix primary and secondary colors). Also, pay attention to logos. In a project that calls for more than one T-shirt, pair a maroon shirt that has mustard-colored text or graphics with an all-yellow shirt. And as you place them together, remember that precision doesn't matter in terms of the angle of the logo. If you get the chance, turn the logo on its side. *Note:* There's no need to find T-shirts exactly like the ones used in this book; even if you do, your version of each project will, happily, be unique.

Scissors Deconstructing is the first step in rebuilding a T-shirt and, in some projects, the only step—so if there's one tool you need, it's scissors. Multipurpose scissors will do the job, but it's a good idea to shell out the bucks for a new pair (a pair that's been used to cut paper

or chop the ends off green beans is going to be too dull for a T-shirt). In my experience, haircutting scissors (even the drugstore ones that cost $13 to $15) work great. They have sharp-pointed tips that can be used to snip or poke holes with accuracy and short blades for a tight turning radius (they're the Mini Cooper of scissors). You can splurge on a pair of the fancy spring-loaded, bent-handled shears that can be found in sewing departments—they're excellent for cutting long, straight lines, but they don't handle the curves (or other tiny detailing) as well. I have a wide range of these "weapons of mass deconstruction" in my stockpile, but you really don't need more than one pair for any of the projects in this book. Once you find the right scissors, keep them sharp—don't use your T-shirt scissors for anything else.

Razor Blade An alternative to scissors, a razor blade does make certain techniques—slashing in particular—very easy. The result is a very rough-looking edge achieved with the utmost control. For safety purposes, it's best to use a razor in the form of a utility knife or box cutter with replaceable blades. Or you can use a pen knife (a small X-Acto®) for very delicate detailing. Both are available at art stores, and hardware stores stock the larger ones. I actually use just a single blade, taped around the edges, to get really close to the fabric.

Another alternative is the **rotary cutter** (it has a circular blade and it looks a lot like a pizza cutter, but smaller and much sharper) and **cutting mat**. The

the anatomy of a t-shirt

Some terms to know for cutting instructions: The *hem* is that inch or so of fabric folded under and sewn in place at the bottom of (almost) every T-shirt. In *Generation T* projects, you won't be sewing hems, just using the existing ones.

A *seam* is where two edges or panels of fabric are sewn together, as at the shoulders of a T-shirt. Most T-shirts don't have side seams.

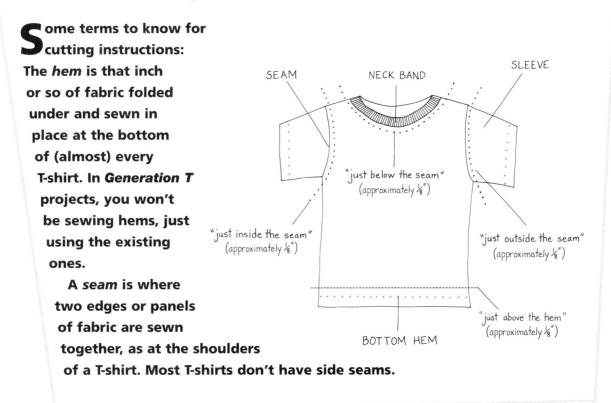

SEAM   NECK BAND   SLEEVE

"just below the seam" (approximately ⅛")

"just inside the seam" (approximately ⅛")

"just outside the seam" (approximately ⅛")

"just above the hem" (approximately ⅛")

BOTTOM HEM

rotary cutter is fast (great if you're cutting a lot of fabric in a short amount of time) and smooth (no jagged edges from opening and closing scissor blades), but you may not have as much control (cutting around three-dimensional shirt sleeves). The cutter takes a little bit of practice, but once you master it, you can do some serious slicing and dicing.

Seam Ripper It's another tool of deconstruction—especially useful in those cases where you've accidentally sewn all four sides of your pillow before stuffing it. Removing seams with a pair of scissors can be clumsy, and you run the risk of damaging the fabric. A seam ripper is easy to stow, comes with a cap for safe storage, and is surprisingly versatile. Use the inside blade to rip a seam open and use the outside (the dull side) of the blade to loosen a stitch or pull a length of thread through to the other side of the fabric without tearing it. While it's not absolutely necessary that you own one, I have to admit I carry mine ("Old Red") around in my handbag—you never know when a deconstruction opportunity might present itself. (As long-legged as I am, I often have to take the bottom hems out of a pair of pants before I wear them—and sometimes that happens to be the second after I buy them!)

Needles These are essentially straight pins with a small hole (the "eye") in one end to hold a length of thread. Though there are about a dozen different types of needles, 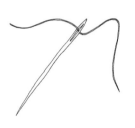 to as many different types of sewing projects (quilting, beading, darning, etc.), you can easily get by with a pack of the *multipurpose needles* called "sharps."

Ballpoint needles are very similar to sharps but have rounded tips that are duller and will penetrate between the yarns of the knitted fabrics instead of through them. (Any sewing or craft store carries them.) The same goes for sewing machine needles. You can use a multipurpose needle for most sewing projects, but a ball-point needle is best for jersey knit fabric.

Some projects here call for an *embroidery needle.* This is much larger than the traditional hand-sewing needle, with a much longer eye to accommodate the thicker embroidery thread.

Thread Thread is sold on cylindrical plastic spools of varying sizes and comes in many different colors. *Poly-cotton blend,* an all-purpose thread, boasts superior strength and elasticity, making it preferable when sewing jersey or other stretch fabrics (T-shirts!). *Cotton thread* is fine, though slightly more prone to snapping. Of course the real punks used *dental floss,* easily found in the aisles of a pharmacy or behind the counter of a corner deli.

Embroidery thread, sold in loops called skeins, also spans the color spectrum—it's used for decorative and other visible stitching. Each strand of embroidery thread is made of six smaller strands that can be separated before use if a design calls for a more delicate stitch.

Straight Pins Not always necessary, but always helpful. I definitely recommend using them for the more complicated projects. And feel free to use them anytime during a project to help you keep the pieces together. A pin is a thin  piece of metal with a sharp point at one end and a flat head on the other used to temporarily fasten fabrics together. I personally like the straight pins with colored plastic balls as heads—they're easy to grasp, and they're also easy to spot if you happen to drop some. Nickel-plated pins are great when you have a nasty spill because you can clean them up quickly with a magnet. The downside: They stick to anything magnetic.

Safety Pins Somewhat of a hybrid, the safety pin is both a functional tool and a decorative accessory. (Imagine safety pins occupying that overlapping space in a Venn diagram.) Safety pins  wrap around and close up so there's no exposed point, and they're always handy as a quick-fix device when a button pops off your pants or a spaghetti strap snaps. In *Generation T,* I use them in place of seams, to expand a seam (and show some skin), or to add a disco sparkle.

Punk Pins Sometimes called buttons, but not to be confused with those that close a shirt or button-fly jeans, these 1"-round pins decorate sweatshirts, back- pack straps, hats, and T-shirts. They are customized variations of the safety pin and add the personality of the wearer to the design. Use them strategically to gather a bodice, ruche a sleeve, attach a strap, or make a faux pleat. Or, in the same spirit of self-expression, you can use a *fancy brooch* or a *barrette* (clasp a rhinestone barrette around a tank top strap for a very flashy corsage).

Tailor's Chalk For any project (especially the more complicated ones), chalk is a great help in marking measurements. Tailor's chalk is square-shaped and its edges can be filed or sharpened for clean marking. (It also comes in pencil form for making finer lines.) Chalk markings can be removed with a plastic brush that often comes attached to the casing. If you plan to make a number of projects, be sure to have both light and dark chalk on hand to show up on dark and light T-shirts, respectively. *Note:* Regular chalkboard chalk works, too (use an old toothbrush as an eraser), though it's harder to make it hold a point.

your space or mine?

Make sure your workspace is a place where you can spread out—find a spot on the floor or a large table. Even though your bed or living room couch has a nice flat surface, don't risk an accidental snip into that vintage quilt or the nice new slipcover! And the space you're sewing in should be well lit—you won't strain your eyes and I guarantee the end result will be better!

Ruler Besides being useful for measuring fabric length, it's used here in several projects as a straight edge—as a marking or cutting guide.

Measuring Tape Also called tailor's tape, it's a flexible, ribbon-like ruler. Straighten it out to get height, inseams, and arm length measurements or wrap it around you to get bust, torso, waist, and

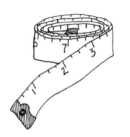

hip measurements. If you don't have a measuring tape on hand, use a piece of ribbon or string (it should be flexible but not stretchy) to measure around you. Then, pinching the measurement point on the string between your fingers, lay it against the piece of fabric and mark. Or, if you need a number, simply lay the length of string against a straight ruler.

Cardboard This is the cutting mat for the thrifty (and environmentally friendly). Recycle the panels of an old cardboard box as a cutting surface or slip them between layers of a T-shirt to prevent cuts

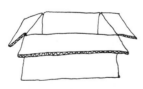

from going through both the front and back. You can use cardboard as thick as that from a corrugated packing box or as thin as that from a cereal box.

Stuffing Originally cotton or wool, stuffing is now most commonly found made from synthetic polyester and is used for puffing up pillows, chair cushions, dolls, and stuffed animals. The key to stuffing is to start

by pushing small bits into the corners of the project before filling out the main body.

Batting It's the stuffing of quilts. It comes in rolls of polyester, cotton, or wool. Polyester batting wins the popularity contest for its resistance to moths and mildew and its resilience (most polyester batting will

return to its original shape after washing). It's also available in a variety of thicknesses and is nonallergenic.

mastering the basics

T hink you know your T-shirt just because you wear it every day? Think again. Before you make your first cut into the shirt, make sure you learn its parts, how it was originally put together, and, most important, the pinning and stitching techniques you'll use to put it back together. Study the shape, the seams, the hemmed edges. How many years do surgeons study anatomy, practice sutures, and review cases before they hit the operating table? Luckily, in the world of T-shirt surgery, these skills can be mastered in an afternoon.

All projects in *Generation T* are rated 1 to 5 according to the degree of difficulty in completing them. Anything rated a 1 or a 2 means there's no sewing involved and is stamped with the **no sew** seal. But really, most of the projects are fairly easy. Many projects are rated a 4 or 5 *only* because it takes longer to make them, thus increasing the patience factor. Never let a rating of 5 discourage you. If you like it, make it.

Measurements When refashioning a T-shirt, you have the opportunity to make it fit perfectly— that's one of the main benefits of personalizing. You're not just custom designing, you're custom fitting, so it's important to know your measurements—your widest, narrowest, longest, and shortest parts. And, once you've got the numbers, always remember to "measure twice, cut once"—this woodworkers' mantra, repeated by my father during many a shared design project, applies to fabric, too. Be patient, because you can always cut more, but it's harder to put fabric back once it's gone.

Take your bust, torso, waist, and hip measurements with tailor's tape. To measure your bust, always measure around the widest part, unless otherwise noted. In this book, measuring your torso means measuring around it, just below your bust. When I say to measure your waist, it doesn't mean the narrowest part—your "natural waist" (up around your belly-button). I mean where you wear most of your clothes—you know, about 2" to 3" below your belly-button, depending on the length of your torso.

Try on your project after every step in order to get the best fit possible. I can't stress this enough. If you're doing "fuzzy math" with your measurements (it's okay,

bust _____

torso (beneath bust) _____

waist _____

hip _____

I was an English major, too), this is the only way to ensure you've got the right size.

Pinning Putting a pin through some fabric sounds easy enough, but there are a couple of things to keep in mind. When joining two pieces of fabric, place the pins perpendicular to the direction you'll be sewing in, especially if you're using a sewing machine—otherwise you run the risk of snapping the needle and jamming your machine. You can also use pins as marking tools (for measurements) when you're out of chalk, or to hold together an unsewn project for fitting purposes.

Threading the Needle Before you stitch, you need to master the art of threading. Getting thread through the eye of a needle can be the toughest part. I've definitely had my moments, brow furrowed, eyes crossed, tongue poking out in concentration, and nothing to show but frayed ends. But cheer up, once you get it, the rest is cake.

Technique #1: Beginner's Method

Measure a piece of thread about the length of your arm. Draw one end of the thread through the eye of the needle. (If you're having trouble, cut a clean end with your scissors and wet it on your tongue.) Double the thread over itself and tie the two ends together in a knot. I recommend using this method if

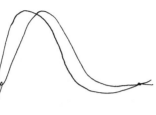

you're just starting out—having the double thickness in your stitches makes for strong, reinforced seams. And you don't have to worry about the thread slipping off the needle every time you pull a stitch tight.

Technique #2: Single Thread

Instead of drawing the thread all the way through the needle, pull it only halfway down the other length of thread. Tie a small knot at the tip of the longer end. This is the more professional method—most hand sewing is done with a single thread except for button sewing.

Knotting the Ends

Whichever threading method you use, you have to knot the end. Take the end of the thread(s) and make a loop. Then draw the end through the loop and tighten. Repeat, layering the second knot over the first.

the stitches

These are the hand stitches you'll need to complete the projects in *Generation T* that are not **no sew**. You'll use the running stitch, the backstitch, or the whipstitch to sew simple side seams; a zigzag stitch or a whipstitch to sew hems or other seams that require horizontal stretch; and finally, use cross-stitches for extra strength and decorative purposes.

When the instructions say "make a ¼" seam," or "leave a ¼" seam allowance," this means you should sew your line of stitches ¼" in from the edges of the fabric. If this is your first time sewing, try practicing the stitches on a scrap piece of fabric before you hit the big time (a.k.a. the projects that require sewing). You'll also need to review how to finish your stitches (see page 17). Even if you're lucky enough to have a sewing machine at your disposal, don't skip these lessons. Most of the hand stitches convert directly to sewing machine stitch options; when they don't, I give the machine stitch alternatives.

Running Stitch This tiny, even stitch is one of the easiest and quickest to do, and often the first stitch a sewer learns. (On a sewing machine, it's called a straight stitch and is the most useful—it's a strong stitch that's reinforced by a second thread coming from the bobbin.) For *Generation T* projects, you'll use the running stitch to complete seams. Here's how you do it:

1. Pick up a small amount of fabric (about ⅛") with the point of your needle.

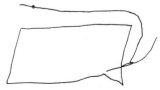

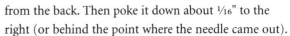

2. Working from right to left, weave the needle in and out of the fabric at about ⅛" intervals until there are several stitches gathered onto it.

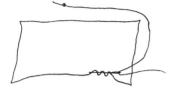

3. Pull the needle through and repeat steps 1 and 2. (The result will look like a series of dashes.) Keep your stitches small and even. If you're feeling self-conscious about uneven rows of stitches (you shouldn't —they've got character), draw a chalk line to sew over.

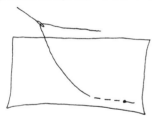

Note: A **basting stitch** (knotted only at one end) is a loose and temporary running stitch you'll use for gathers (see page 18).

Backstitch (or Running Backstitch)

This is the strongest and most durable of the hand stitches, and though it looks very much like the running stitch, it has better hold. (It's the hand stitch equivalent of the sewing machine straight stitch.) Do it like so:

1. Pull your needle up through the fabric,

from the back. Then poke it down about ¹⁄₁₆" to the right (or behind the point where the needle came out).

2. Pull the needle up through the fabric ⅛" to the left of the first stitch.

3. Poke the needle into the fabric right next to the beginning of the first stitch, making another ¹⁄₁₆" stitch.

4. Repeat steps 1 through 3, moving backward and then forward (that's why it's called the backstitch) until you've reached your endpoint. *Note:* The stitches on the underside will be twice as long as those on the top side.

Whipstitch This strong overedge stitch is used to join two flat edges together. It's the one I use most in my hand sewing because it offers room for horizontal give, which complements the stretch of the T-shirt fabric—and it's quick and easy to do. I also use it in place of a running stitch when I don't have enough fabric to leave a full ½" seam allowance. (There is no direct translation of the whipstitch for sewing machines, but I often use the machine zigzag stitch for its stretching potential.) Follow these instructions:

1. Starting about ⅛" from the fabric's edge, pull your needle from back to front through both layers of fabric.

Use a zigzag stitch when you want the fabric to give or stretch a little—for example, on anything that needs to stretch over your head, hips, or around your bust. The running stitch, in which all stitches are sewn parallel to the direction of stretch, may snap when you try to stretch the fabric, especially if it's made with regular cotton thread.

2. Moving from right to left, continue pulling the needle from back to front, bringing the thread over the edge of the fabric, as shown. Pull thread snugly against the edge.

3. Repeat steps 1 and 2 (moving about ¼" to the left along the edge with each stitch) until you're done. Your stitches will look slanted.

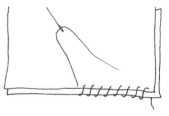

Zigzag Stitch More difficult to do by hand than on a machine, the zigzag is a flexible stitch that offers some stretch without your having to use elastic thread. It's good to use around waistbands and tube tops. Try your hand at it:

1. Pull your needle up from the back of the fabric about ½" from the edge.

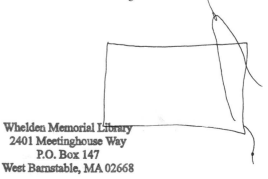

2. Moving from right to left, poke the needle down on a diagonal, ¼" from the edge.

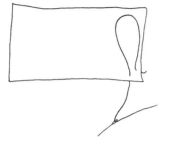

3. Pull the needle back up just next to the spot where you went down in step 2.

4. Poke the needle down ½" from the edge on a diagonal perpendicular to the stitch you completed in step 2, as shown.

5. Pull the needle back up just next to the stitch in step 4 and repeat steps 2 through 5 until you reach the end.

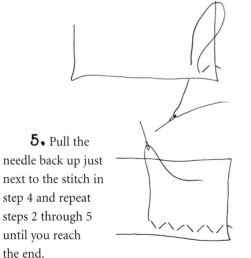

A zigzag pattern will develop on one side of the fabric as you go, and a polka-dot pattern on the other.

Cross-stitch Both practical and decorative, the cross-stitch is used when you have a visible seam or want to add a little sumthin'-sumthin' to a project. To accentuate the pattern, use colorful embroidery thread. (Though there's no equivalent cross-stitch on most sewing machines, there are many other decorative stitches to choose from that offer similar effects.) By hand, it goes like this:

1. Starting ¼" from the edge of the fabric, pull your needle up through the fabric (A) and then poke it back down (B) on a diagonal along the edge you're sewing, about ½" to ¾" from your point of origin.

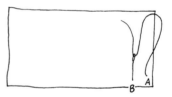

2. Pull the needle back up (C) at a point directly above B and ¼" to the left of A. (*Note:* You'll have created a short stitch on the underside that is perpendicular to the edge of the fabric you're sewing.) Moving from right to left along your seam, continue making diagonal stitches, parallel to the first in step 1. (These are the beginning of your crisscrosses.)

3. When you reach the endpoint, pull your needle up through the fabric directly above the last stitch. Working left to right, go back over your previous path, making diagonal stitches that form Xs over the row you made in steps 1 and 2.

4. Continue moving from left to right until all your crisses are crossed (and you're back where you started).

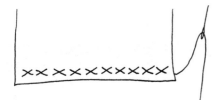

Boxed Cross-Stitch It's basically just what it sounds like: a cross-stitch in a box. The box adds strength and support when securing, or tacking, strips of fabric (such as wraparound ties or straps) to the body of a project. (On a sewing machine, you can get a similar effect by sewing a straight stitch in a square.) To box and crisscross, follow these steps:

1. Make two stitches (perpendicular to the edge), pulling your needle up into the fabric and poking it down at the opposite edge. (The distance between these stitches will vary with each project, but as a guide, try to come about ¼" from the edge of the piece of fabric you're tacking down.) You will have cre-

ated a single diagonal stitch (half of a cross-stitch) on the underside of the fabric.

2. Make the third side of the box by completing the crisscross on the underside, pulling your needle up at the bottom of your first stitch, as shown, and poking it down at the bottom of your second stitch.

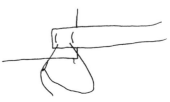

3. To complete the box, pull the needle up at the top of the first stitch and poke it down into the top of the second stitch.

4. Pull your needle up through adjacent point (A) and poke it down through the diagonal point (B).

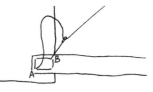

5. Pull the needle up at the original point (C) and poke it down on the diagonal point (D) to complete the crisscross.

Finishing a Stitch To finish any of the stitches above in a secure knot (except for the temporary basting stitch), make a single small backstitch on the wrong side of the sewing project, leaving a small loop. Send the needle and thread through the loop and pull it tight. Repeat the stitch a second time, on top of the first, and pull it tight again. Trim your thread with scissors to about ½".

(back)

adding style

Drawstrings are those all-important elements on your baggy pants and strapless items that keep things on the up-and-up and prevent you from baring all.

To make a drawstring: Simply cut a strip between 1" and 2" wide from a T-shirt. (Or cut the hem off the bottom of a T-shirt so you take advantage of the existing reinforced seam.) Tug on it a little to stretch it to maximum length. For a sturdier drawstring, cut a 3"-wide strip. With the wrong side of the fabric facing up, fold the edges into the center of the drawstring (the strip is now 1½" wide), fold the folded edges together (the strip is now ¾"), and sew the open edge closed with a zigzag stitch or whipstitch. Of course, you can also use ribbons, shoelaces, leather strips, twine, thin rope—you name it—for a drawstring.

tee trivia

Putting the "T" in Haute: The first couture T-shirts were designed in the 1960s. Dior led the pack with a striped velvet tee in his 1962 collection. Close on his heels, other designers interpreted the T-shirt in crepe, pearls, and gold lamé.

A drawstring is no use without a drawstring casing. Often the hem of the original T-shirt can become the casing for the drawstring of a new T-skirt or tube top. At the center or side of the hem, snip a small hole through only the top layer of fabric—instant transformation from hem to casing. If there is no hem readily available, simply fold over ½" to 1" of fabric (depending on the width of your drawstring) at the edge and stitch it in place. Snip a hole as described above.

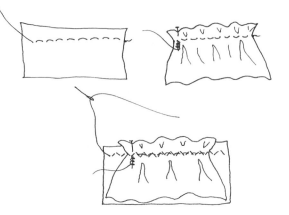

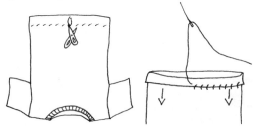

To thread a drawstring: Imagine the drawstring is a length of thread and attach a safety pin to one end as if it were the needle. Push and pull it through the length of the casing with the motions of an inchworm.

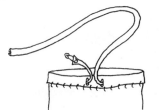

Gathers are used to draw in fabric for a soft, feminine fit. They traditionally adorn waistlines, shoulders, and cuffs, and give the bottoms of skirts a ruffled billowy effect (think ruffled cap sleeves and tiered skirts). Use a loose running (basting stitch) along the edge of the fabric you plan to gather. When you reach the end, remove the needle but hold on to the thread while gently pushing the fabric in the opposite

direction (against the knot). Insert a straight pin at the unknotted end of the gather and wrap the thread around it to keep the fabric from slipping and flattening. With right sides together, lay the gathered piece against the piece of fabric to which it is to be attached. Adjust the gathers so they are evenly spaced and both pieces are the same size. Pin them in place and stitch the layers together to hold the gathers permanently. Once the gathers are secure, remove the basting stitch with a seam ripper. For more control over the spacing of your gathers, you can add a second row of basting stitches, ¼" from the first, inside the seam allowance.

tee trivia

More than two billion T-shirts are sold worldwide each year.

(When making gathers with a sewing machine, use a long straight stitch and loosen the upper tension slightly. Secure one end of the thread with a straight pin as above and then gather by pulling the bobbin thread.)

Ruching is a type of gathering, but I like to differentiate it because it's not permanent (it can always be untied). Instead of gathers, you create two parallel casings (or one single casing) to run a drawstring (or two) through, gathering the fabric and securing it by tying the drawstring ends.

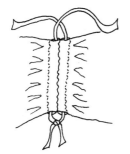

Our **no sew** version requires a drawstring strip to be used like a piece of thread and "sewn" through holes along a length of fabric, with the strips tied at the end.

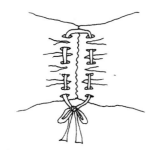

Appliqués are pieces of one material that you sew or pin to the surface of another. You can liven any piece of plain fabric by attaching a patch (in a contrasting

color) in the shape of a square, circle, star, heart, skull, letter, and so on. First arrange the cutout shape on the surface of the background material and pin it in place. Then sew around the edge of the shape using a small running stitch no more than ¼" from the edge (no more than ⅛" if the shape is very small), and remove the pins. Though it's harder to keep your stitches neat, you can also use a zigzag or overedge whipstitch, as shown on the heart, above.

coloring outside the lines: adding embellishment

From ribbons and lace to bike chains and rock pins, detailing and accents are the icing on the cake. When you're looking to embellish your T-shirt beyond the traditional *Generation T* slashing and tying, think creatively and you won't have to look very far. Buttons, beads, sequins, pins, ribbons, Grandma's brooches (or her pearls, for that matter!), game pieces, old shoes,

continued on page 22

dyeing, batiking, printing, bleaching

Generation T is about deconstruction and reconstruction, focusing on transforming the nongraphic aspects of a T-shirt with already existing graphics. But there are ways to refashion the *surface* of a T-shirt. Beyond markers and photo transfers, you may want to experiment with some of the following techniques. These are only the briefest of introductions, and be forewarned, they require a lot more setup than the projects in this book, not to mention more start-up.

Tie-dyeing You've probably tried your hand at making a homemade Grateful Dead–style shirt at least once—summer camp, fifth-grade art class. But if you were like me, your skill wasn't perfected and your shirt came out blah: the blue, turned out gray; the red, pink; the yellow was barely visible.

So who was the first successful T-shirt dyer? No one really knows, but the tie-and-dye technique can be traced back to several regions of the world. Since at least the eighth century, Japanese have practiced *shibori*, using labor-intensive resist processes to create intricately patterned kimonos; in India the technique is known as *bandhana*; and in Peru, Indonesia, and sub-Saharan Africa, it's a deeply rooted art form.

If you've never tie-dyed, give it a try. Simply twist, fold, knot, or scrunch a T-shirt (preferably a white one) until it's a tight bundle, and tie it with rubber bands and string (the tighter you tie, the more elaborate the design). Submerge the bundle in a dye bath (often made by mixing boiling water, dye, a fixative, and salt) for about a minute. You can choose to immerse it in one dye or a couple of dyes, or immerse half in one and half in another. Rinse the dyed bundle in cold water, squeeze out the excess water, and hang it up to dry.

Screenprinting Bold. Defined. In-your-face. Screenprinting (also called silk screening or serigraphy) is a technique commonly used on band T-shirts and was popularized in the 1960s by the Pop Art movement (think Andy Warhol's *Marilyn*). To achieve this silhouetted look, you need the following tools: a frame, a piece of nylon or polyester fabric large enough to fit the frame, a stencil, ink, a rubber blade, and, of course,

celebri-tee corner

"Meet T-shirt Author **Bart Simpson**" reads the banner in an episode of *The Simpsons,* in which Bart goes from living-room floor DIYer to T-shirt mogul. Using blank T-shirts and permanent markers, he catches the eye of a gift entrepreneur. Bart's T-shirt slogans: "Wish You Were Beer," "Wake Me When It's Recess," and "This T-Shirt Sucks."

a T-shirt. The stencil should have the desired motif cut out of a sheet of plastic or heavy cardboard larger than the T-shirt. Stretch the piece of fabric over the frame and secure it with staples or tacks. Lay the entire frame on the T-shirt and tape the stencil flat on the framed fabric (you now have a sandwich with the frame in the middle). Spread ink evenly across the screen with the rubber blade. Lift the screen, and the stenciled image will have transferred to the T-shirt. Check out *www.moma.org* and search "screenprint" for detailed interactive instructions.

Batiking It's similar to tie-dyeing because of the dip-and-dye factor. But instead of binding fabric to keep the dye out, you use wax resist—think one step beyond those kindergarten crayon-and-watercolor multimedia masterpieces.

To batik, heat wax in a double boiler and apply it with a brush or dropper to an extremely dry piece of fabric. The dye will not penetrate the areas where the wax is applied. Wait for the wax to cool (this process quickens with the help of a fridge or freezer) and then immerse the fabric in a dye bath. Hang it up to dry. To melt off the wax, submerge it in a solvent or iron it between paper towels or newspapers. Your batik is complete.

Bleach Pen Yep, the Clorox® Bleach Pen®, normally used for spot-bleaching pesky stains, has now been embraced by the crafting community as a new DIY tool.

Cut a stencil out of cardboard or plastic and lay it on a dark-colored T-shirt. Insert another piece of cardboard inside the shirt to prevent seeping. Apply the bleach gel sparingly over the stencil and wait for it to dry. Rinse the shirt in a vinegar-and-water solution to neutralize the bleach and reduce fabric damage. Wash it before wearing. (You can skip the stencil image entirely and draw a design or write a freehand message on the T-shirt with your pen.) The result has faded vintage appeal—and is actually very basic batik in look.

Here's your bleaching color guide: Blue shirts turn lighter blue or white; red turns pink or white; brown and green turn tan; black and navy blue turn orange.

tee trivia

Ready for some competition? There were only two competing T-shirt brands in 1945: Hanes and Union Underwear, a.k.a. Fruit of the Loom. Since then, dozens of T-shirt manufacturers have joined the fray, among them Jerzees, Jockey®, and American Apparel.

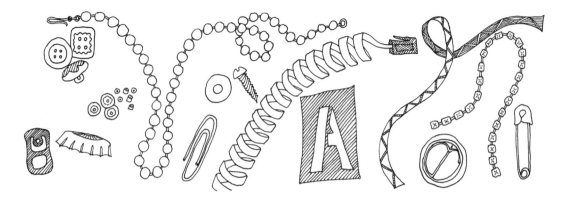

bottle caps, soda can tags, telephone cords, stencils, and hardware (rivets, screws, nails) can all add that special something to your refashioned T-shirt. Remember the paper clip chains you made in fourth grade? Definitely fair game. Check out department store clearance racks, hit the local thrift or secondhand spots, garage or stoop sales, and don't be afraid to trash-pick! In true scavenger style, don't rule anything out.

Once, on a late-night stroll down Broadway, I happened upon a group of trendy-looking scavengers picking through some garbage bags outside a shoe boutique—it was a gold mine of left-footed shoes labeled "development samples." Oh, I sampled, all right, grabbing as much as I could and stuffing it into my bag. When I got my found treasures home, I cut them up—leather and canvas straps to use on tank tops and halters, little metal clasps and pieces of Velcro that could be used functionally or sewn on as decoration. Even a short chain of rhinestones embedded in one of the platform shoes was salvageable.

Another time, I uncovered a ratty sweater while rooting through a 50¢ bin at a sidewalk sale. The sweater was nothing special, but it was trimmed with orange- and gold-flecked tiger-embroidered ribbon—

perfect! I kept the ribbon to dress up a pillow I was working on (and used the rest of the sweater to stuff it).

My best find so far was truly a family affair. When my grandfather finally retired, at age eighty-nine, it was our job to dismantle his old office machine repair business. I clipped some typewriter keys to personalize a shirt and then sketched out a design for a matching belt. My sister took some keys to make cuff links for our brother (his initials) and a tie tack for my dad, and my dad made bracelets for each of the girls.

When it comes to embellishments, I'm giving you full license to think outside the suggestions in this book. Find your own add-ons and put your personal signature on each project you create. Thumb your nose at Fifth Avenue, and become the rogue fashionista you were meant to be!

"I'm a black-belt shopper, always have been. I still get a little thrill whenever I see these two words: FREE and DISCOUNT."

—Oprah Winfrey

man vs. machine: care and handling

Though knit jersey is one of the most durable, low-maintenance fabrics, keep in mind that once you've had your way with a tee, you're no longer dealing with a garment made on a heavy-duty, industrial-strength sewing machine. If your sewing is on the more delicate side, I recommend using the delicate cycle in a washing machine or even washing by hand.

zen and the art of t-shirt deconstruction

The Zen law of crafting asserts that there are no mistakes—only variations. What seems like an error may be the hottest new trend. Once I accidentally slashed through both the front and back of a T-shirt, when I had intended only to make an opening in the back. It became a challenge: Do I safety-pin the hole in the front or sew it? Do I add a piece of fabric, poke holes, and lace it back together with a ribbon? Or do I just slash it even more? I went from not knowing what to do to idea overload. Each solution brought me a completely new design, reminding me that the learning was in the process, not necessarily in the end result.

So, if you make a mistake, don't stress it; see it instead as an opportunity. Jot it down in the sketching area at the back of the book, Do-It-Yourself, page 254.

bring it on

T-shirt reconstruction combines recycling and innovation—you're remaking something old into something new. It's especially appealing (and empowering) to those of us raised in a world of mass production and limited resources. You're saving the world one T-shirt at a time and letting people know it. The tee itself is a personal billboard; your reconstruction of it is your graffiti tag. It's one part impulse, one part ego, two parts subversive, and it's art.

If you're a beginner, you may want to follow the instructions in the next chapters very closely, but if you're a more seasoned refashionista, you can treat them simply as guidelines.

Even when you follow the instructions for each project faithfully, it's guaranteed that no two projects will be exactly alike—you'll be spontaneously creating your own variations as you work. Approach the T-shirt as just a piece of fabric, and there an infinite number of ways to interpret it. And once you have a handle on some of the basic techniques taught here, you can use those skills to develop your own designs.

So, don't ask what your T-shirt can do for you; ask what you can do for your T-shirt. And then Do-It-Yourself.

keep your shirt on

Draw your scissors from your holster; here are 13 projects that involve customizing, cutting, clipping, tying, and pinning—as much deconstruction as you can do and still call it a T-shirt.

T-shirt doesn't have to be retired when it gets a hole, or when styles shift and baggy tops or tight, tummy-baring numbers are passé. It just needs a status check—and some resuscitation. If it's got holes, make more. If it's too baggy, nip and tuck. If it's too short, lengthen it; too long, chop it.

Along with the sheer physical satisfaction (what with the cutting, slashing, snipping, and all), refashioning a T-shirt is emotionally fulfilling, too. It's about recycling (satisfying your inner environmentalist), and it's about not buying things you could make (satisfying your inner anticonsumerist). And, as if you needed more, you're also exercising those First Amendment rights, freedom of speech and freedom of artistic expression—never overrated.

Now here's the big question of this chapter: Why transform a T-shirt into a T-shirt? Now here's the answer: For *you*. No matter what store you go into, you won't find anything with *your* look—*your* signature. (Unless, of course, your name happens to be Von Dutch, Baby Phat, or . . . Old Navy?) Brand-name designers base their styles on reports from "fieldworkers" who hit the streets and "gather data" to find out what trends are hot. But seriously, what does a mass-marketing trend consultant know about the styles that speak to you?

Who isn't sick of wearing someone else's logos? Do you still have that old T-shirt with the letters G-A-P across the front? Here's your chance to change it up a little. Take those three letters and rearrange them. Maybe you're actually a fan of the . . . um . . . P-G-A? Okay, bad example. But let's try another: Calvin Klein. Scramble the letters for "Neck Villain." All right, all right, but you get the picture— no one else will have the same phrase on their Calvin Klein original. Represent yourself.

Millions of identical classic tees get cranked out from factory assembly lines each year. They get checked by Inspectors 9, 32, and 57 to make sure there's nothing "irregular" about them. Your goal is to flunk inspection, to be as irregular and irreverent as you can be. Here's your chance to be different, to make a statement. "No comment" is not an option.

The way you use your scissors (and needle and thread) can be a political, social —and of course, personal—statement. So get creative, get ready to customize and make it yours. Wear something no one else has. A department store has about 15 of the same items on a rack. A boutique has three. How about sporting an original— a true one-of-a-kind?

scoop, there it is

A perfect intro to T-shirt DIY, this design is a flashback to *Flashdance*. It doesn't get any easier than this. You've probably already made this shirt at some point in your life, but didn't understand its significance. This is the gateway drug of T-shirt deconstruction—it makes you want to do more. So pull up your leggings, spread the glitter on thick, and put another dime in the jukebox, baby.

LEVEL 1

Lay the T-shirt flat and cut off the edge of each sleeve just above the hem stitching (for a raw edge). *Optional:* Cut off the bottom of the shirt just above the hem.

---
ingredients
---

1 T-shirt
(not fitted)

scissors

Cut out the neck band.

Try on the shirt. If the neck isn't scooped enough (for best effect, it should slide off one shoulder), take off the shirt and widen the neck by cutting out more fabric. It's smart to snip a little at a time, trying on the shirt after each alteration. It may seem tedious, but the end result is worth it.

variations

o totally '80s and gather the bottom of the shirt (if it's large enough) into a knot at your hip. Eighties pop fashion— there ain't nothin' better.

r, just cinch it to accentuate your positives. Both of them. See project 37, Bodice Snipper, for the **no sew** gathering.

ake a deep scoop in the back of the T-shirt and attach T-shirt strips to the top of each shoulder and tie at the back of your neck. It's a quick fix if you cut so much fabric from the neck that it won't stay on.

(back)

tees in the movies

Flashdance (1983): Jennifer Beals, as Alex Owens, inspired a whole generation of off-the-shoulder DIY T-shirts that extended far beyond the dance (and welding) world.

slash 'n' sash

One part sash. One part swift kick in the pants. And just a pinch of femininity. You don't have to be a kung fu master to achieve this ass-kicking style. Channel Bruce Lee, Uma Thurman, or go old-school with the Karate Kid. Oh, but without the karate. No board-breaking, no wasted money on lessons, and no fly-catching with chopsticks. Just two T-shirts and one afternoon, and you'll have instant fighter instincts. **LEVEL 4**

Lay the smaller T-shirt flat and cut out the neck band. Cut off the edges of the sleeves and bottom just above the hem stitching.

Choose the side on which you'd like your T-shirt to tie and make a 4" vertical cut from the bottom of the shirt. Set aside.

ingredients

2 T-shirts (preferably one fitted, one XL in different colors or patterns)

scissors

straight pins

needle

thread

Lay the larger T-shirt flat. Cut off the bottom just above the hem stitching. Then cut approximately 5" from the bottom of the shirt through both layers, creating a tube. Snip through one layer so that you're left with one long strip.

Using a whipstitch, sew the shirt and strip together along the pinned edge. (Start at one end of the dangling tie and work your way around the base of the shirt, ending with the second end of the dangling tie.)

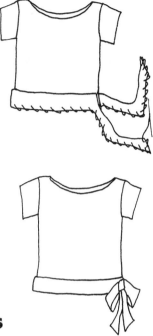

Fold the strip in half so you'll have a long strip about 2½" wide. Cut the ends on a diagonal, as shown.

Remove pins, fold the strip down, slip the shirt on, and tie it up. Wax on. Wax off.

variations

Tuck in ½" of fabric along each side of the open edge of the folded strip, including the ends, and pin.

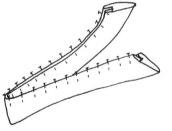

f you want to play with the karate look, use different colors from other T-shirts to upgrade your belt status.

Pin the pinned edge of the strip along the lower edge of the smaller T-shirt, matching the middle of the strip with the uncut side of the shirt. Let the excess strip length dangle.

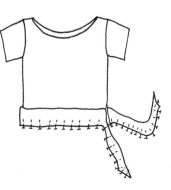

se the same belt technique to add a bow around the neck of a shirt. See project 1, Scoop, There It Is, for the base.

brokenhearted

This is the perfect way to get out some aggression over that recent breakup. Even better if the T-shirt you slash was left behind by that not-so-special someone. Put on Bon Jovi's "You Give Love a Bad Name" or your own favorite breakup ballad, and go to town with those scissors. Just don't get too carried away, or you'll end up with a pile of T-shirt confetti. **LEVEL 1**

Turn the T-shirt inside out. With a piece of chalk, sketch the shape of a heart across the torso of the shirt. *Optional:* Cut out the neck band and cut off the sleeve ends to make the edges raw.

Draw parallel lines horizontally inside the outline of the heart, approximately 1" apart.

Insert the cardboard flap between the layers of the shirt and, being sure to cut through only the front panel of the shirt, slash along the chalk lines.

cardboard

---

ingredients

---

1 T-shirt (preferably fitted)

tailor's chalk

cardboard flap

scissors (or razor blade)

Turn the shirt right side out and layer it over a tank top or another tee.

variations

ollow the same chalk-and-slash technique with any pattern you want—sketch it out on a piece of paper first and then transfer it to a T-shirt. For instance, another of my **no sew** favorites is one I call Super 'Fly. Transform the front of your plain T-shirt into a butterfly tank top the way Clark Kent changes into Superman (or a caterpillar into a butterfly!). Wear over a multicolor tank to brighten your wings.

tee trivia

"**B**ack in *my* day": In 1942 a package of three T-shirts cost only $1.10!

fringe benefits

Introduced by Native Americans of the Great Plains, celebrated by flappers in the Roaring Twenties, and revived by the hippie generation, fringe has seen its fair share of changing times. Pick your look, pick your era, and shimmy to your heart's content. **LEVEL 1**

tee trivia

The famous "Anarchy" T-shirt worn by Sex Pistol bassist Sid Vicious fetched an amazing $6,000 at Sotheby's in 2001.

ingredients

- 1 T-shirt
- scissors

Lay the T-shirt flat and cut out the neck band just below the seam. Cut off the edges of the sleeves just inside the hems, and cut off the bottom of the shirt just above the hem.

Starting from the raw edge, cut fringe strips 1" wide and 2" long around the end of each sleeve.

Cut fringe strips 1" wide and 3" to 4" long around the bottom of the shirt.

variations

Native American fringe has always been up to the job of multitasking. Besides looking great on the tribal dance floor, fringe was used to wick away water from wet leather, as camouflage to obscure the human silhouette, and as a way to brush off hungry insects. Moccasin fringe was even thought to hide footprints made on dirt trails. And, perhaps most important, fringe was the essential fix-it item—in a bind, strips were cut to replace a broken shoelace or hair tie, or to reattach a necklace or bracelet. Note to today's DIYers: T-shirt fringe is no different.

ut strips all the way up to the shoulder seams, so the sleeves are 100% fringe.

ie a knot at the bottom of each piece of fringe to give it more weight.

r, thread large-holed plastic beads onto each piece of fringe and tie knots beneath them to keep them secure—an option reminiscent of the braids and beads sported courtside by the Williams sisters.

pleasantly punk

I t's all sugar 'n' spice on the outside to casually complement your girly grit. Bring on the cute, wholesome ruffles, but remember, the T-shirt you choose can make all the difference—it can be plain and pastel for a more traditionally sweet look or boy grunge for an edgier, more against-the-grain look.

LEVEL 2

ingredients

- 1 T-shirt
- ruler
- scissors
- tailor's chalk

Lay the T-shirt flat and cut out the neck band. Then cut 3" from the bottom through both layers, creating a tube. Snip through one layer so that you're left with one long strip.

Cut three 1" strips along the length of the strip and set them aside. *Optional:* Cut the strips from another, contrasting T-shirt to spice up the color and design. Or use real ribbons in place of the T-shirt strips.

Measure 3" from the bottom of the shirt and mark a line across the shirt with chalk. Along the line, make small (½") incisions 2" to 3" apart around the circumference of the torso.

Note: Make an even number of incisions so that the drawstring ends will come out on the same side.

Starting at the center front, weave one of the 1" strips in and out through the incisions.

Measure and mark 2" from each sleeve end and make small (½") incisions 1" apart around the circumference. (Again, make an even number of incisions.)

Cut one of the remaining strips in half. Weave one half strip in and out of the holes in one sleeve. Repeat with the other sleeve. When you pull the ends like a drawstring, you'll get a "puffy sleeve" effect. Tie the ends in small bows.

Repeat step 3 around the neckline, measuring, marking, and cutting 1" from the edge. Weave the last strip in and out of the neck incisions. Taking care not to pull the ends (the neckline should not be gathered), tie them in a small bow.

Put on the shirt and gather the drawstring at the waist. Tie it in a bow. (Bet you didn't see that coming.)

celebri-tee corner

In the 1950s and early '60s, **James Dean, Marlon Brando,** and **Elvis Presley** delivered a triple dose of T-shirt sex appeal onscreen and onstage, turning the garment into an icon of rebellion.

ruffle and tumble

Got a chip on your shoulder? Good. Add some ruffles. Now, to really ruffle some feathers, pick a shirt with an inflammatory slogan, be it political, personal, or just plain rude. **LEVEL 3**

ingredients

1 T-shirt (fitted)

scissors

measuring tape

1 or 2 T-shirt scraps (small, in contrasting color to base T-shirt)

tailor's chalk

needle

thread

straight pins

Lay the shirt flat and cut off the sleeves just outside the seams.

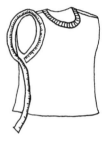

Measure the circumference of one armhole and add 2" to determine the size of the sleeve ruffle.

On the T-shirt scrap material, draw and then cut two matching crescent-shaped pieces whose length (along the straight edge) is equal to the measurement determined in step 2.

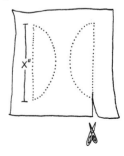

4 Baste along the straight edge of each crescent. Gather the fabric evenly over the thread, shortening the length by about a third.

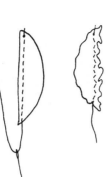

variations

Cut out the neck band for a more rough-edged look.

5 Center the stitched edge of the ruffled crescent along the top of each armhole and pin in place, right side to right side, as shown. Using a whipstitch, sew along the pinned edge.

Use scraps from two different T-shirts to have unmatched ruffles.

6 Remove pins, fold out the ruffles, and wear.

tee trivia

Sixty-two percent of Americans claim to own more than 10 T-shirts. That's 1.5 billion tees, and if you lined them up, they'd circle the globe 34 times.

"The T-shirt will never go out of fashion because it's already beyond fashion."

—*Elle* magazine

comfort corset

It's clearly corset inspired, but made out of T-shirts, the comfort level, like Spinal Tap's amp, "goes to 11." Granted, it won't give you a 10-inch waist, but it won't crush your spleen, either.

LEVEL 2

ingredients

- 1 T-shirt (M)
- scissors
- ruler
- tailor's chalk

Lay the T-shirt flat. Trim about 2" off the ends of the sleeves and about 1" off the bottom of the shirt (just above the hem stitching), to use in step 5.

Cut out the neck band to about 2" from the shoulder seams at each side.

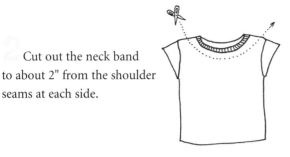

Put on the shirt and gently tie the two ends together at the top. Trim the ends as necessary.

(back)

On the back of the T-shirt and starting at the sides of the neckline, cut a scoop measuring about 10" down from the center of the neckline.

(back)

variation

Layer a fitted tank top underneath and wear the Comfort Corset backward, with the lacing in the front.

About 1" from the new neck edge, snip four small incisions evenly spaced along both sides of the scoop, as shown.

(back)

Thread the 1" hem from step 1 (cut into a single strip) through the small holes, criss-crossing from bottom to top as if you were lacing a shoe. *Optional:* Use a ribbon or a T-shirt strip of a contrasting color.

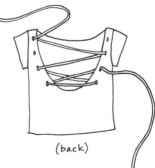

(back)

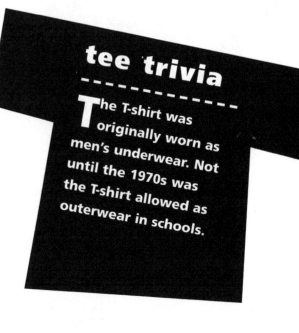

tee trivia

The T-shirt was originally worn as men's underwear. Not until the 1970s was the T-shirt allowed as outerwear in schools.

it's a cinch

Hipsters in your neighborhood driving up the rent? Show 'em what real hip is with this belly-baring number. Ruche up the fabric by pulling some strings and you'll up your flesh factor, too, keeping pace with the party. **LEVEL 4**

ingredients

- 1 T-shirt
- scissors
- needle
- thread

Turn the T-shirt inside out and lay it flat. Cut about 2" from the bottom of the shirt through both layers so the shirt falls at waist or hip level. (Save the piece you cut off for step 6.)

Cut around the neck band to create a scoop neck. (See project 1, Scoop, There It Is.) *Optional:* Also cut the sleeves for a rough-edged look.

Cut vertically up the front of the shirt, slightly off center.

With right sides together, sew the two cut edges with a running backstitch 1" from the edges.

Press the seam open and sew each of the 1" seam allowances (flaps of fabric) to the shirt with a running stitch or whipstitch (creating two parallel drawstring casings).

Cut a drawstring from the scrap piece cut in step 1 and, starting at the bottom, thread it up one casing to the neckline, then back down the other casing.

Turn the shirt right side out and try it on. Pull both drawstring ends to ruche the fabric as high as desired and tie the ends together.

variation

ry using a contrasting color strip from your scrap pile as the drawstring. Or, use a colorful ribbon in place of the drawstring.

mix 'n' match

Fire up a little love for that great American pastime. This design is a nod to my old baseball practice jerseys—we used to call them, quite aptly, our "sleeves." You can play, too, simply by cutting the sleeves off any tee and replacing them with sleeves from a tee of a different color. It's a sporty look that's very giftable because it's so versatile—it can be dressed up or down, it can be for a girl or a guy. Let's play ball! **LEVEL 3**

ingredients

- 2 T-shirts (same size but different colors)
- scissors
- straight pins
- needle
- thread

Turn both T-shirts inside out and lay them flat. Cut out the neck bands and cut off the sleeves of each shirt just inside the seams.

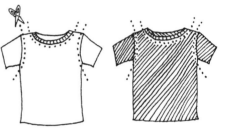

Turn the sleeves of one shirt right side out. Lay one sleeve inside the body of the other shirt so the cut edges meet at the armhole. Pin it in place, matching the underarm seams.

Using a whipstitch, sew along the pinned edge, leaving a ¼" seam.

Repeat steps 2 and 3 with the second sleeve.

Sew the neck band from one T-shirt inside the neck of the other, using a whipstitch.

Remove all pins and turn the shirt right side out.

variations

ttach the remaining set of sleeves and neck band to the remaining T-shirt torso, and you'll have Mix 'n' Match's alter ego.

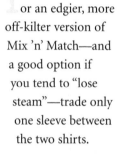

or an edgier, more off-kilter version of Mix 'n' Match—and a good option if you tend to "lose steam"—trade only one sleeve between the two shirts.

o make the Indie rock ringer tee, swap the neck-pieces and use the sleeves of the second T-shirt to edge those of the first, as shown.

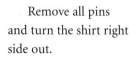

shoulder slash

It's off the shoulder, but not quite. It's showing some skin, but nothing scandalous. It's a little teasing game of peekaboo with that tattoo on your shoulder. And it's good ventilation, besides.

LEVEL 1

ingredients

1 T-shirt
scissors

Lay the T-shirt flat and cut out the neck band.

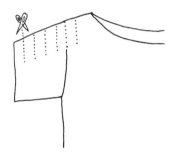

Starting about a third of the way from the neckline down to the end of the sleeve, cut 1"-wide vertical incisions halfway through the width of the sleeve. This will create small peekaboo strips.

Repeat on the second sleeve. Easy, or what?

pin-up

Debbie Harry (yes, of Blondie fame). This is one girl who brought safety pins into top fashion. Her look reflects true gutter punk—a style of pure practicality, originated by people who simply didn't have the cash to buy new clothes. And lest you think it was all for show, Debbie Harry was a practical punk rock girl. She wore safety pins on the bottom of her skirts to keep the hem weighted down. If only Marilyn Monroe had been so utilitarian. **LEVEL 2**

ingredients

- 1 T-shirt
- scissors
- 1 box safety pins (small or medium)

Lay the T-shirt flat and cut out the neck band.

Cut off about 1" of fabric (along the shoulder seams), from the neckline down to the ends of the sleeves.

Note: If the tee is already too tight on your biceps, just make cuts down the tops of the sleeves, without removing any fabric.

Use the safety pins to join the cut edges together, placing the pins about 2" apart. The larger the safety pins, the more skin you show . . . naturally.

halftime

Half of one T-shirt plus half of another T-shirt equals a whole lotta fun. Get ready, sports fans. I like to use this design format to celebrate (and illustrate) some of the most famous rivalries in sports—Packers vs. Bears, Red Sox vs. Yankees, or Lakers vs. Spurs. Or, if sports aren't your thing, match cheerful with dark, white with black, or pink with army green. Pair two of your boyfriend's threadbare tees to make him a brand-new one.

`LEVEL 3`

Spread both T-shirts flat and cut vertically up the center of each, from bottom hem to neck, through both layers so that each shirt is in two pieces.

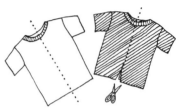

Take the left side of one shirt and match it to the right side of the other shirt, overlapping the fabric ½" along the cut edges. Pin in place.

---

ingredients

---

2 T-shirts
(same size but
different colors)

scissors

straight pins

embroidery needle

embroidery thread

Using an external cross-stitch, sew the two halves together along the pinned edges. Remove the pins and wear it, or gift it.

celebri-tee corner

Guys get in on the safety pin action, too. **Johnny Rotten** and **Sid Vicious** weren't originally making a fashion statement with their shredded clothes—they sewed on patches to cover holes in a threadbare shirt, and when the cloth around the patches wore away, they'd pin together what was left.

variations

ith the two remaining halves, make a matching (yet opposite) T-shirt (or save them for the **no sew** version below).

or a **no sew** version, grab a box of safety pins (small or medium) and attach the two halves with horizontally placed safety pins (1" to 2" apart).

or a less revealing version, overlap the rough edges, front and back, and attach them with vertically placed safety pins.

se just one T-shirt, cut vertically up the center, and sew the two halves back together again. It's a Humpty Dumpty success story.

ode to the mullet

Inspired by the mullet, it's business in the front, party in the back. When I saw this design in a shop, I was attracted by the sexy skeletal look (no, I don't mean skeletons are sexy, so don't go getting anorexic on me). The part of me that's fascinated by human anatomy saw a fantastic rib-cage effect in the overpriced tee. **LEVEL 5**

ingredients

1 T-shirt
scissors
(or razor)
1 flap from a
cardboard box
tailor's chalk
straight pins
needle
thread

Lay the T-shirt flat and cut off the hemmed ends of the sleeves. Cut off the bottom of the shirt just above the hem stitching and cut out the neck band.

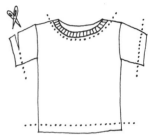

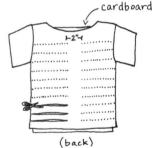

cardboard

(back)

Flip the shirt over and insert the cardboard between the front and back layers. Leaving the center 2" untouched (mark it with chalk to make cutting easier), make an even number of horizontal cuts 1" apart along the back of the shirt, from mid-sleeve to the bottom of the shirt on both sides of the center margin. The slits should reach from the chalk mark all the way to the sides of the shirt.

At the sides of the shirt, snip through *every other* strip made by the cuts in step 2, starting with the top strip.

(back)

Down the center margin, mark and cut 2" horizontal slits between the strips you snipped through in step 3. Make your cuts at the vertical midpoint between those strips.

(back)

Now comes the tricky part. Take one of the snipped strips and thread it through the slit you made in the middle, drawing it up through the hole from inside the shirt. Without twisting it, pin it to the side of the shirt it was originally cut from. Repeat the process with the strip on the opposite side of the center margin.

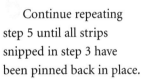

(back)

Continue repeating step 5 until all strips snipped in step 3 have been pinned back in place.

(back)

Using a whipstitch, sew along each of the pinned areas, removing the pins as you go. *Optional:* Use safety pins instead of stitches for a **no sew** version.

tees in the movies

Dream a Little Dream (1989): The two Coreys (Feldman and Haim, as Bobby Keller and Dinger) team up to slash their jeans, mousse their hair, and, yes, shred their T-shirts for the first day of school.

Try on the tee and hit the town.

chapter 3

get militant

Here are 21 tank tops that are less shirt, more glory—they're low on fabric, high on style.

What are you showing off in a tank top that you're not showing off in a T-shirt? Your arms, your shoulders, how 'bout those biceps—otherwise known as your "guns"? The tank top, with its turret-toting name, gives you full creative license to exercise your Bill of Rights and *bare* those arms. You can bare a lot or a little, go with thick straps or thin, one strap or two, highly structured or a little rough around the edges. And this chapter has all that. It's an explosion of tank tops—athletic, elegant, boyish, flirty, skimpy, hip, and fun. Pick your style and express yourself.

In an interview in 1984, Madonna bared her arms in a sleeveless slashed T-shirt and declared her dream "to rule the world." As a global pop culture icon, she has, in a sense, achieved that goal. But she didn't get there by playing it safe. She raised eyebrows, ruffled some feathers, went against the cultural norm, and left controversy in her wake. If you think about it, even our founding fathers were revolutionary punks, going up against the authority of their day. (And how much more DIY subversive can you get than sticking a feather in your cap and calling it "macaroni"?)

You've already challenged the shape of the conventional T-shirt if you've made any projects in chapter 2. Now take it up a notch and go sleeveless. Among the tank style pioneers are the jock, the punk, the beach bum, the ballet dancer. Even if you're none of the above—or a jocky-punky-beach-bummin' ballerina all rolled into one—you too appreciate the freedom of movement the tank top offers. The tank inspires confidence and draws attention to your amazing arms and shoulders—shapely, skinny, tanned, or tattooed.

But sculpted biceps won't get you everywhere—this is where your self-expression and creativity come in. You're trying new things in this chapter. Besides taking off the sleeves, you're adding hoods, twisting fabric, braiding straps, punching holes, and texturing with mesh—all without spending a dime or buying into a corporate vision. And it almost goes without saying, these tank tops are dangerously sexy . . . but that's another kind of power altogether. So . . . what's in your arsenal?

Living in a material world, the Queen of Pop sets her own style standards.

classic punk

We're getting back to the roots of punk with this one. Deconstruct it. Let your rebelliousness punch through—really, it's a positive thing here. By the time you finish this one, you'll be ready for anything— even "Anarchy in the U.K."

LEVEL 3

ingredients

1 T-shirt
(S, M, or L)
scissors
straight pins
ruler
needle
thread

1 Turn the T-shirt inside out and lay it flat. Cut off the sleeves just inside the armhole seams. *Optional:* Cut out the neck band just below the seam.

2 Depending on your size and the size of the shirt, cut 3" to 6" off each side, through both layers of fabric. (If the shirt is already fitted, simply cut off the sleeves and stop there for some **no sew** lovin'.)

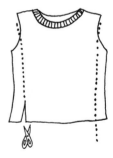

variations

Stick a pin horizontally in each side of the tank to mark where the bottoms of the armholes should be. Using a whipstitch, sew up each side, stopping at the pin.

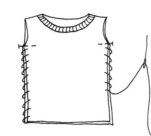

Turn the shirt right side out, remove the pins, and wear.

xperiment with the width of the neck opening—you can leave the neck band intact (more traditional, and more popular among the guys) or scoop it out wide, gathering the sleeves with punk pins. Remember that you can always cut more, but you can't put the fabric back.

se external cross-stitching (in a contrasting thread color) for a decorative look, right.

The photograph of John Lennon, with arms crossed, in a refashioned New York City T-shirt (sleeves removed), is so iconic that you can now buy a T-shirt imprinted with the image.

shoulder chic

Lay the T-shirt flat and cut off the sleeves just inside the seams.

You know how delis name sandwiches after people (like the Joe DiMaggio Hero or the Kevin Bacon BLT)? Well, if this project were a sandwich, I'd name it after myself. This smart cutaway tank represents everything I like a project to be: It's incredibly easy to make and innovative. You work with the existing structure of a T-shirt to create a shape that's new, exciting, and sexy. Shoulder Chic showcases—what else?—the shoulders (which just *happen* to be one of my favorite features). **LEVEL 1**

Measure and mark 2" along the neck band from where the neck band and shoulder seam meet. Draw a line from each chalk mark to the bottom of each armhole. Repeat on the back.

---

ingredients

---

1 T-shirt
(S, relatively fitted)

scissors

chalk

ruler

"I'm not a label whore. I've always loved shopping and fashion, but I also made a lot of my own stuff, ripped up clothes, sewed things on."

—Halle Berry, actress and DIY diva

Cut along the chalk lines from the bottom of the armholes to the neck band. Then cut around the edge of the neck band (through the shoulder seams on both sides) until you reach the corresponding chalk marks on the back.

Cut along the two chalk lines at the back from the neck band to the bottom of each armhole.

Remove excess fabric and try on the tank to show how chic your shoulders can be.

variation

or a **no sew** halter top version, cut through the fabric still connected to the back of the neckpiece. Then cut from the bottom of one armhole across the back of the shirt to the bottom of the other, creating a slight scoop.

outer lace

I f the word *lace* makes you think of rocking-chair grandmas, this laced-up reincarnation will make you think rock 'n' roll. Though (no joke) I know a very hip grandmother who refashioned a handprinted "World's Best Grandma" tee from her grandkids to create this punk rock design. "World's Best Grandma"? Try World's Best-*Dressed*. However, this tank top is not for your average grandma and, given its potential for sexy skin-baring, might just be . . . um . . . slightly more suited to your figure. **LEVEL 2**

1 Lay the T-shirt flat, and cut off the sleeves just inside the seams. Cut off the bottom 2" above the hem (save fabric for step 5).

2 Depending on your size and the size of the shirt, cut 3" to 6" off each side, through both layers of fabric. (The best way to determine this is to try on the shirt and measure the amount of extra fabric you can pinch at the sides.)

---

ingredients

- 1 T-shirt
- scissors
- ruler
- straight pins

3 Use a pin on each side of the shirt to mark where the bottoms of the armholes should be.

4 Starting at one of the pins, use the point of one scissor blade to poke small holes 1" to 2" apart through both layers, down the side of the shirt, 1" from the edge of the fabric. Repeat on the other side.

5 To make the laces, cut two 1"-wide strips from the length of the shirt bottom cut off in step 1.

Optional: Use ribbon in place of the T-shirt laces.

6 Starting at the underarm, thread one strip through the two top holes, then weave each end in and out of the holes, criss-crossing as you go—as if you were lacing a shoe. Tie the two ends in a bow at the bottom of the shirt.

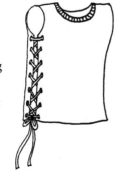

7 Repeat step 6 on the opposite side.

8 Remove the pins and try on your tank, adjusting the "laces" as needed.

variations

try your hand at lacing up other parts of the tank: Slash down the front and back of the tank and lace it back up. Or just cut a 5" slit down the middle of the neckline and lace it up.

for another **no sew** version, close up the sides you cut open in step 2 with horizontally placed large safety pins. Cut out the neck band, make a 2" to 3" slit down from the center of the neckline, and reattach the fabric with three small safety pins.

lace age

I call this the third-date shirt. Not
only is it DIY sexy, it's the physical
manifestation of giddy anticipation.
You're bursting at the seams (the
ones that already exist, since
this project is **no sew**).
And, if all goes well,
someone may unlace
you at the end of
the night.

LEVEL 2

1 Lay the T-shirt flat and
cut out the neck band just
below the seam. Cut off
the sleeves just outside the
seams.

2 Cut out 1" to 2" of fabric
along the top shoulder seams
from neckline to armholes.

3 Leaving a
¾" margin along the top,
poke an equal number of
holes about 1" apart on the
four shoulder edges.

---
ingredients
---

1 T-shirt
(preferably fitted)
scissors

Now poke holes about 1" apart along the front and back of the neckline, also leaving a ¾" margin from the edge. Cut a 1" strip off the bottom to use as a drawstring.

Starting at the top of one armhole, thread the drawstring (from step 4) through the holes in the front and back of the shirt as if you were lacing up a shoe.

tees in the movies

Crossroads (2002): In her big-screen debut, the princess of pop, Britney Spears, and cohorts cut and slash a few T-shirts for the road. And click on the DVD bonus feature: a no-sew T-shirt tutorial so you can make one just like Britney's at home. (Though it's really just a variation of Outer Lace, project 16.)

variation

se ribbon, shoelaces, or T-shirt strips in a contrasting color instead.

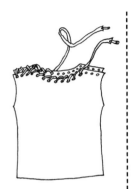

When you reach the edge of the neckline, continue threading one end of the string through the holes along the front of the neck as if you were doing a whipstitch. Take the other string and do the same through the holes at the back of the neck.

When you get to the other end of the neckline, resume the shoelace technique. At the end of the shoulder tie the two drawstring ends in a bow.

Try on and adjust laces as necessary.

ties to die for

I made this shirt for a friend who's tough but ultra feminine. She reads Bukowksi wearing jeweled cat-eye glasses and crowd-surfs at Leftover Crack shows in her slip dress and Mary Janes. This tank is the lady version of the Classic Punk, project 14. Think of it as punk rock lite. And pop open a girlie beer. **LEVEL 2**

----

ingredients

- 1 T-shirt (S or M)
- scissors

1. Lay the T-shirt flat and cut off the bottom hem just above the stitching. Then cut four 1"-wide strips off the bottom to use as drawstrings. (Each string needs to be at least 18" in length.)

   Optional: Ribbon can replace the T-shirt strips in this project. And shoelaces, too—don't forget the shoelaces!

2. Cut off the sleeves just inside the seams. Cut out the neck band just below the seam.

3. About 1" from the shoulder seam, poke small holes 1" apart along both sides of the seams.

4 Take one drawstring and thread it through one hole closest to the armhole, poking the end from the outside of the shirt to the inside. Thread the string in and out of the holes on one side of the seam, like a running stitch. When you get to the neckline, cross the string under the shoulder seam to the other row of holes and thread it in and out alongside the seam. Repeat on the other side.

5 Pull the ends of the strings to gather the fabric and tie them in a bow.

6 Starting at the bottom side of the shirt, poke two 6" to 7" vertical lines of parallel holes about 1" apart (the center margin should be about 1½").

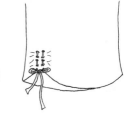

7 Thread one of the strings through the holes, using the same technique as in step 4. Pull the ends to gather the fabric, and tie them in a bow.

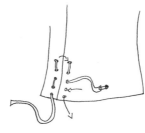

8 Repeat step 7 on the other side. Slip it on and tie it up.

tees in the movies

Sid and Nancy (1986): Gary Oldman, as bassist Sid Vicious, sleeveless and crude, brought gutter punk new esteem.

fermez la ruche

This shirt is an act of defiance against the laundromat demons. (They can't shrink it because you are the one pulling the strings here.) Like raising a stage curtain, when you tug on the side strings, you're gathering up the fabric in order to showcase the scenery behind it. **LEVEL 4**

ingredients

- 1 T-shirt
- scissors
- straight pins
- needle
- thread

Turn the T-shirt inside out and lay it flat. Cut off the sleeves just inside the seams.

Cut off the bottom hem just above the stitching, then cut two 1" strips off the bottom of the shirt to use as drawstrings.

Cut vertically up each side, from the bottom of the shirt to the bottom of the armhole.

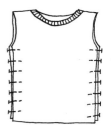

With the inside still facing out, pin the cut edges together, 1" in from the sides. (Do this on both sides of the shirt.)

> "Like jeans, T-shirts are the objects of desire for teenagers, BoBos (bourgeois bohemians), snobs, men, women, everybody."
>
> —designer Sonia Rykiel

5 To attach the front and back panels of the shirt, sew along the pinned area, using a short (⅛") running stitch.

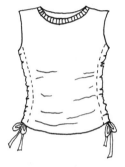

6 Fold the 1" seam allowance open and pin it flat. Using a backstitch, sew along the outer edges to create two tunnels (drawstring casings). Repeat on the other side. Remove pins.

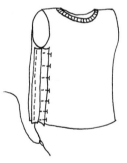

7 Starting at the bottom, thread one drawstring up one tube and back down the tube next to it. Repeat on the other side with the other drawstring.

8 Turn the shirt right side out and ruche the fabric by pulling the two ends of the drawstrings. Experiment with how much skin you want to show and tie the ends at the bottom.

variations

If you want the drawstring casings to be visible, don't turn the shirt inside out in the first step.

Create a **no sew** version by adapting the technique used in project 18, Ties to Die For. Punch holes and thread the strings all the way up the side of the shirt instead of just 6" or 7" up.

Make the ruching casings on only one side of the shirt (leaving the other side plain) for a hiply disheveled look.

it's my party

no sew

and i'll tie if i want to

(You would tie, too, if it happened to you.)

LEVEL 2

tee trivia

Mul-tee-purpose: During war times, the T-shirt has been used as a towel, a smoke mask, a hat, a tourniquet—even a white flag.

ingredients

- 1 T-shirt
- scissors
- ruler
- tailor's chalk

1 Lay the T-shirt flat and cut off the sleeves just inside the seams. Cut out the neck band and then cut a deep V neckline in the front and back. (To make an accurate V, cut a 5" slit down from the center of the neck hole, and then cut a diagonal line from the 5" point to the sides of the neckline.)

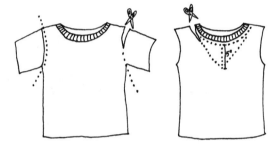

2 Being sure to cut all the way through both layers of fabric, mark and cut two triangles (about 4" high) down one side of the shirt, creating a zigzag shape.

3 Repeat on the opposite side.

Tie the three points of the front zigzag edge to the corresponding points on the back, closing up the sides of the shirt.

Try on and make any adjustments (tighten or loosen a knot, make the neckline plunge deeper, etc.).

variations

ometimes the zigzags just aren't long enough to tie in knots. If that's the case, poke a hole 1" in from the points of the zigzags and then cut short strips to tie each of the pairs of points together at your side. (Also try leaving the neck band intact.)

ut horizontal fringe instead of zigzags along the open sides of your tank, and tie it closed—less skin, very hot.

safety first

Not only do safety pins hold this tank top together, but it's conveniently shaped like a life jacket (in a cute, unbulky way). Thankfully, it's more flattering than those orange preservers and can be made in an array of contrasting colors. *Do* try this project at home. *Do not* try to use it as a flotation device (or you will be one sorry wet punk).

LEVEL 1

---
ingredients
---

2 T-shirts
(L, in same or
different colors)

scissors

ruler

1 box safety pins
(small or medium)

Lay one T-shirt flat and cut off the bottom hem. Then cut an 8"-wide strip from the bottom (or middle, if the graphics are more interesting), creating a tube.

Cut through the tube along one side to make one long strip. Fold it in half horizontally, wrong sides facing in.

Repeat steps 1 and 2 on the second T-shirt.

Lay the two folded strips next to each other— vertically so that the cut ends are nearest you.

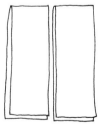

Pin the inside edges of the top layers together with safety pins, starting about a third of the way from the top and spacing the pins about 1" apart.

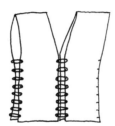

Flip the strips over and do the same for the back layers.

With safety pins, attach the outside edge of the back layer to the outside edge of the front layer, starting about a third of the way down and spacing the pins about 1" apart. Repeat on the other side.

Slip the tank on—careful that no earrings or other piercings get caught in the mesh of safety pins! Add or subtract safety pins (for more or less coverage) as desired.

nstead of having safety-pin "seams," whipstitch the edges together.

or variety, use smaller safety pins on the sides and larger ones in the front and the back—or vice versa.

Never mastered the art of lacing up your shoes? Safety pins, the Velcro of T-shirt redesign, to the rescue! It's hard to imagine that a device that is essentially nothing more than a diaper pin could have such a pivotal and lasting role in the fashions of the potty-trained demographic. And yet it has endured.

diamondback

*F*act: A diamondback snake sheds its skin up to four times a year. *Fact:* With this shirt on your back, you'll have shed some fabric . . . and some inhibitions. *Fact:* Rattlesnakes hunt at night, sensing the heat of their prey. *Fact:* In your diamondback tank, you, too, are nocturnal and make temperatures rise as you flirt your way around the bar. *Fact:* Rattlesnakes subsist on a diet of rodents and other small animals. Not you—sexy and serpentine, you're a man-eater. Get back! This one's got fangs.

`LEVEL 2`

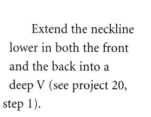

Lay the T-shirt flat and cut off the sleeves just inside the seams. Cut out the neck band just below the seam.

Extend the neckline lower in both the front and the back into a deep V (see project 20, step 1).

From the hem to the point of the V-neck, make a vertical cut up the center of the shirt, through both front and back layers.

---
ingredients
---

1 T-shirt (M or L)

scissors

ruler

tailor's chalk

4 Into each of the cut edges (through both layers), mark and cut triangles 3" to 4" long and 1" to 1½" wide, creating a zigzag edge. On the opposite edge, cut mirror-image triangles, that is, point to point and V to V. (The pattern will look somewhat like a backgammon board.)

5 Starting at the point of the V-neck, tie the top strip on the right and the top strip on the left together in a knot. Continue until the bottom two strips have been knotted together.

6 Flip the shirt over and do the same on the back.

7 Try it on and make adjustments for fit by tightening or loosening the knots.

tee trivia

The T-shirt became a canvas for free expression in the 1960s, when silkscreen inks were developed. This technology paved the way for a new phase of T-shirt slogans ("I'm with Stupid," "I RAN the concession stand at THE BOSTON MARATHON") and images (the Rolling Stone tongue, the Superman icon).

a beautiful day in the 'hood

You're feeling antisocial, with your headphones plugged in and your sweatshirt hood pulled over your head. So, what happens when you're having one of those days, but it's sunny and pushing 90°? I believe a girl should still be able to hide if she feels like it, no matter the weather. Here's to the angst-ridden girlz in the 'hood—so black-eyeliner tragic and misunderstood.

LEVEL 4

---

ingredients

---

2 T-shirts (1 fitted, 1 larger)

scissors

measuring tape

straight pins

needle

thread

Lay the fitted T-shirt flat and cut out the neck band and sleeves, just inside the seams. Then measure the circumference of the neck hole and divide by 2.

Turn the larger T-shirt inside out and flatten it on its side so the front and back of the shirt are the new "sides," as shown. Measure the number from step 1 (x) along the bottom length of the shirt and mark with a pin. From the same corner, measure about 14" up the side and put a pin.

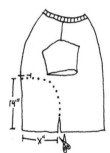

3 Mark and then cut (through both layers of the T-shirt fabric) an exaggerated convex "J" shape from one pin to the other, separating the fabric for the hood from the rest of the shirt.

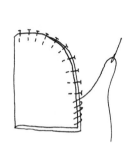

4 Pin and, using a whipstitch, sew the curved edges of the "J" together.

5 Cut through the fold on the long straight side and turn piece right side out. This is your hood.

6 Pin the center of the back of the hood to the center back of the neckline of the fitted T-shirt. Continue pinning until the two corners of the hood nearly meet at the center front of the neckline.

7 Sew around the pinned area with a whipstitch. Or use a zigzag stitch if the neck opening is snug and needs to give, or stretch, a little. Remove pins. Hide inside.

variations

by not sewing completely around the curved edge, you can create a wide lavish collar instead of a hood.

the fairytale version: Use red T-shirt fabric to make the hood and—*voilà!*—Little Red Riding Hood. Use green, and you're Robin Hood.

instead of adding fabric to make the hood, cut some away for a **no sew** peekaboo tank: Using a coffee can lid or a round coaster as a pattern, trace and cut three half-circles (3½" in diameter) down each side of the shirt, spaced about 2" apart. (You can increase the number of circles you cut down the sides by making them smaller and closer together.)

For variety, tie a small piece of ribbon around each of the 2" of fabric between the circles.

put me in, coach

Get ready to play, today. The pitcher's throwing the funny stuff, but you're seeing the ball so clearly you can make out the stitching. Or is that a tank top getting pitched your way? This project uses very visible cross-stitches—inspired by the stitching on a baseball. Step up to the plate and hit this one out of the park. Take a spin around the bases—just don't run with scissors! **LEVEL 4**

tee trivia

Political Par-tee: Thomas E. Dewey was the first presidential candidate to flaunt his slogan on a T-shirt ("Dew it with Dewey") during the 1948 election.

1 Lay the T-shirt flat and cut off the sleeves just inside the seams.

2 Cutting through both layers, make an arc at the bottom of the shirt, as shown (this means the shirt will be slightly shorter—2" to 3"—at the sides than at the front and back).

3 Mark and cut on a diagonal line (through both front and back layers) from the bottom of the armhole through the neck band, 2" down from the shoulder seam, as shown. Repeat the diagonal cut on the other shoulder.

ingredients

- 1 T-shirt
- scissors
- ruler
- tailor's chalk
- straight pins
- embroidery needle
- embroidery thread

Overlap the newly cut edges (shoulder pieces on top) about ½" and pin them back together. Using a cross-stitch, sew along the length of the pinned and overlapped edges.

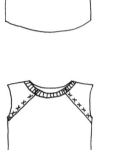

Remove the pins and get ready to rumble.

variations

ew on shoulder pieces using material from another T-shirt in a contrasting color.

o complete the sporty look, cut out a number (if there isn't already one printed on the T-shirt) from your scraps (a sleeve will work), pin it to the front or back, and sew along the edges with a running stitch.

it's a string thing

The appliquéd front of this scoop-necked tank projects a certain groundedness and comfort—think Sunday morning coffee-and-paper routine. The strips accentuate your body's curves, creating a sexy, sophisticated look. But the hanging strands at the bottom give the tank a more playful, deconstructed feel, as if winking at the previous night's revelry. **LEVEL 4**

ingredients

- 2 T-shirts (1 fitted, 1 larger, in different colors)
- scissors
- ruler
- tailor's chalk
- straight pins
- needle
- thread

1 Lay the smaller T-shirt flat, cut off the sleeves just inside the seams, and cut out the neck band just below the seam. Cut off the bottom of the shirt just above the hem stitching.

2 Measure 2" to 3" down from the center of the front of the neckline and cut a curve from one shoulder to the other, through the marked point.

3 Take the larger T-shirt and cut six 1" strips from the bottom of the shirt all the way to the shoulder (through only one layer).

Starting 1" from the neckline edge, pin three of the strips 1" apart at the top of the shoulder of the first shirt. If you want the edges of the strips to lay flat, place them right side down.

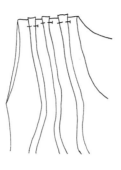

Pin the strips in place following the curve of the neckline, and then down the front of the shirt. Let any extra strip length dangle past the bottom.

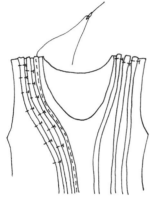

Sew along the pinned areas using a single line of running stitches down the middle of each strip.

Repeat steps 4 through 6 on the opposite shoulder with the three remaining strips.

Remove the pins. Trim the ends of the strips so that the two in the middle are longest (and the two on the ends are shortest), and wear.

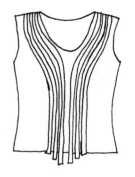

variations

ouble the length of the strips by cutting through both layers of the second shirt (including the shoulder seam) and sew them down the front and the back of the tank top.

ave the second T-shirt for another project and use ribbon instead of T-shirt strips (it'll catch the light much better).

r, for a **no sew** version, use safety pins to attach the strips to the tank.

sew easy

There's no needle and thread necessary for this one, but it's "sew easy" because you use basic in-and-out sewing techniques with T-shirt strips. My version of Sew Easy has sentimental value because I used my first band T-shirt. The first time I washed it, I had made the mistake of putting it through the spin cycle with a lone red sock. Needless to say, it sat in the back of a drawer until I rediscovered it one day (aha!), refashioned it, added a little flair, and reclaimed it (*Sew* easily done!)

LEVEL 2

Lay the small T-shirt flat, cut off the sleeves just outside the seams, and cut out the neck band just below the seam. Trim off the bottom hem just above the stitching.

Measure 2" to 3" down from the center of the front neckline and cut a curve from one shoulder to the other, through the marked point.

ingredients

2 T-shirts (S and L, in different colors)

scissors
(or razor blade)

ruler

tailor's chalk

From one shoulder, mark and cut ½"-long horizontal slits about 1½" apart in three "columns" down the front layer of the shirt as follows: The first column of slits should go straight down from the shoulder, nearly to the bottom of the shirt; the second should be made on a diagonal to the first, ending on the same horizontal plane; the third should start right next to the second, then arc across the torso to the opposite hip.

Note: Make an even number of slits so that when you thread the fabric through, it will end up on the outside.

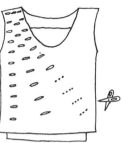

↳ cardboard

Cut off the hem and cut three 1" strips off the bottom of the large shirt.

Take one strip and knot at one end. Starting at the top slit on the shoulder, treat the knotted strip like a needle and thread, weaving it in and out of the slits. Continue down the row of horizontal slits until you reach the bottom. Let the end dangle.

Repeat step 5 for the remaining two strips.

Optional: Use three ribbons instead of fabric strips to add a little shine to the otherwise matte finish of the tee.

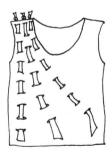

celebri-tee corner

In with the In Crowd: When **Jackie Onassis** was photographed in 1972 sporting casual dark blue T-shirt fashion, everyone knew the tee was here to stay.

heavy meshinery

At its worst, mesh fabric gives me flashbacks to middle school PE with its musty gyms and sweaty "pinnies." At its best, mesh fills me with nostalgia for team bus rides to away games (French braids and pump-up mix tapes), and state championships. It's those memories that make me want to pay tribute to one of the great styles that sports have given us—mesh reconceptualized as civilian streetwear.

`LEVEL 1`

Lay the T-shirt flat and cut off the sleeves just outside the seams.

Insert the cardboard flap between the front and the back of the shirt to prevent cutting through both layers.

Starting at the bottom of one armhole and working toward the other, use the ruler as a guide to mark and cut a series of small horizontal slits (about 1" long) about ½" apart across the shirt.

— cardboard

---
ingredients

- 1 T-shirt
- scissors or razor blade (for a more precise cut)
- 1 flap from a cardboard box
- ruler
- tailor's chalk

"A desire builds up in me to work in materials of waste and softness. Something yielding, with its only message, a collection of lines imprinted like a friendly joke."

—Robert Rauschenberg, artist, Zen master of trash, and hero to a whole generation of T-shirt refashionistas

4 About ¾" below this row, start another one, staggering the slits slightly so they don't line up directly under the cuts made on the previous line (the effect should resemble the pattern of a brick wall).

5 Continue making rows of slits until you've completely filled the space above and below that first series you made in step 3.

6 Flip the shirt over and follow steps 3 through 5 on the back of the shirt.

(back)

7 Layer it over a tank top or bathing suit.

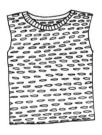

variations

before you start making the slits, cut out the neck band and widen the neckline to create a boatneck.

experiment with the length of the slits—try making 2"- or 3"-long slits about 1" apart.

that's a wrap

I've always been fascinated by kimonos and kimono-style shirts. It seems more natural, somehow, to wrap clothes around us than to pull them over our heads or button them up. The reverse act of unwrapping is elegant and inviting—a far cry from whipping off a shirt and tossing it in the corner. This design implicitly poses the question: Who gets to unwrap you? **LEVEL 5**

ingredients

- 1 or 2 T-shirts (M or L)
- scissors
- ruler
- tailor's chalk
- straight pins
- needle
- thread

1   Lay the T-shirt flat, backside up. Cut out the neck band just below the seam and make a vertical cut through the top layer from the center of the neckline down to the bottom of the shirt.

(back)

2   Beginning at the sides of the neckline, mark and cut diagonal lines about 10" long that meet the vertical cut made in step 1.

3   Cut off the sleeves just inside the seams. Try on the shirt like a vest—you'll most likely need to make the armholes smaller, so mark where you'd like them to end and pin them.

4   Turn the tank top inside out and use a whipstitch to close up the part of the armhole you pinned.

5 Turn the tank right side out again and cut 5" off the bottom. You'll use this piece for the two belt parts.

Note: For a thicker belt, or one in a contrasting color, use a second shirt in a different color, and cut 8½" off the bottom.

6 Cut the strip in half lengthwise so you have two long strips, each 2½" wide.

7 Fold each strip in half lengthwise, wrong side out, and pin along the long edge, leaving the ends open. Sew (with a whipstitch) along the pinned edge. Turn tubes right side out.

8 About 6" up from the bottom of the tank, sew the end of one tube to one edge of the front opening. Then sew the other tube to the other side.

9 About 6" up from the bottom along one side of the shirt, cut a small vertical incision about 1" high (or 2" high if you chose to make a wider belt in step 5)

10 Put on the shirt and wrap one side across your belly. Thread the end of the "belt" through the slit you made in step 9, wrap it around your back, and tie it in front to the other end. Trim the ends so they're the same length when they meet in front.

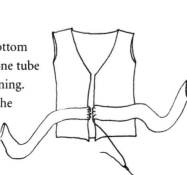

six-pack

Whether you've got a six-pack or a keg, whether you're ready to show off your belly or you need some incentive to flaunt it, this shirt bares your midriff. Wear it over a bikini at the beach or strolling along the boardwalk (or sidewalk—you're not shy). It's also a great materni-tee gift for a friend who's got a bun in the oven—pregnant women look adorable with their bulging bellies on parade. **LEVEL 2.5**

---
ingredients
---

1 T-shirt (S or M)

scissors

ruler

tailor's chalk

needle

thread

1   Lay the T-shirt flat and cut off the sleeves just inside the seams. Cut out the neck band just below the seam. Make a vertical cut through the top layer from the center of the neckline down to the bottom of the shirt.

2   Beginning at the sides of the neckline, mark and cut diagonal lines about 10" long that meet the vertical cut made in step 1.

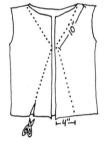

3   Along the bottom, measure 4" from the cut edge and mark. Then mark and cut a diagonal line connecting that point to the cut made in step 2. Repeat on the other side of the bottom of the shirt.

Parallel to the bottom of the shirt, cut 2" into one of the points (making two short flaps), as shown.

Try on your tank and show the world your stuff . . . er, belly.

On the other point, directly opposite the cut made in step 4, cut a 1"-long slit 1" in from the edge and parallel to the bottom of the shirt.

variations

ou can wear this one backward, too, for an open-backed smock look.

Take one of the short flaps made in step 4 and thread it through the 1" slit made in step 5.

ince the sewing is so minimal on this one, you can easily substitute a single safety pin for the small amount of sewing in step 7 for a completely **no sew** version.

Pull the other short flap to meet the first so the ends of the two flaps are back together, and sew them with a whipstitich.

r, for an even easier **no sew** version, skip the last five steps and pin the two points together, overlapping them slightly, with a punk pin or brooch.

greek goddess

Why do Athena and Aphrodite always look so grand in paintings and statues? Because in addition to roiling the heavens and stirring the passions of men, Greek goddesses knew how to drape cloth around themselves. The sensuous folds lounging along the neckline of this tank top will make you look positively statuesque. **LEVEL 4**

---

ingredients

- 2 T-shirts (S and L)
- ruler
- scissors
- straight pins
- needle
- thread
- punk pin, brooch, or sparkly barrette

1. Lay the large T-shirt flat and cut off the hem above the stitching. Then cut two 8" tubes off the bottom.

2. Cut through both tubes to make two long 8"-wide strips, then lay them end to end and sew along the edges to form one long strip.

Lay the small shirt flat and cut off the sleeves just inside the seams. Cut out the neck band 2" below the seam.

Gather up one end of the strip (from step 2) and pin it at the bottom of one shoulder strap.

Loosely drape the strip around the front of the neckline hole to the other shoulder, and tack it in place at the base of the strap with straight pins. Continue wrapping the strip over the shoulder and around the back of the neckline, gathering it and tacking it to the straps.

Use a running stitch to sew the strip to the tank top in four places: in the front and back of each shoulder strap where you pinned it.

Remove the pins and bring the end of the strip over the shoulder. Pin a brooch or punk pin, or clip a barrette around the strip, and let the rest hang down the front of the shirt. Trim any excess fabric.

Arrange the fabric folds just so, and show your allegiance to your sisters of Mount Olympus.

celebri-tee corner

In 1992, *Miami Herald* sports columnist Edwin Pope was so certain of a young tennis player's bleak prospects that he wrote: "If **Andre Agassi** ever wins Wimbledon, I'll eat his T-shirt." When Agassi won the men's singles title a week later, Pope's column humbly queried, "Will somebody please tell me how to eat a T-shirt? Broil it? Bake it? Fricassee it?" and pleaded only that Agassi send him a clean one.

queen of braids

Pippi Longstocking was a DIY kind of girl—independent and self-assured. She had two kooky braids, socks that didn't match, a pet monkey, and an insatiable appetite for adventure. Follow her lead and don't look back. This design is T-shirt tested, Pippi-approved. Two kooky braids: Check. Scraps that don't match: Check. Pet monkey: Fido should do just fine. Insatiable appetite for adventure: Pack your bags.

LEVEL 2

---

ingredients

---

1 T-shirt (M)
scissors
ruler
tailor's chalk
T-shirt scraps
2 safety pins

Flip the T-shirt so the back is facing up, cut off the sleeves (inside the seams), and cut a gentle arc through only one layer from the base of one armhole to the base of the other.

(back)

Flip the T-shirt so the front is facing up. Through the front layer *only*, cut a straight line across from the middle of one arm-hole to the middle of the other.

Cut off the hem and then cut three 1"-wide strips off the bottom of the shirt, through both layers. Trim them to about 30" in length and choose three complementary 1"-wide and 30"-long strips from your scrap pile.

(back)

Pin the ends of three of the strips together and braid them. Repeat with the other three.

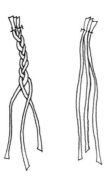

At the center back, about 1" down from the edge, poke two small holes 9" apart.

(back)

From the outside of the shirt, thread the loose end of one braid through one of the holes. Pull it through until you have a 7"-long "tail." Tie that end in a knot. Repeat on the other side with the other braid.

(back)

Snip a small hole in each of the top corners of the front of the shirt, 1" in from the sides.

Try on the shirt, cross the straps in the back, and thread them (inside to outside) through the holes you made in the front. Adjust the length of the straps, remove the pins, and knot the ends. Trim the ends and you're good to go.

variations

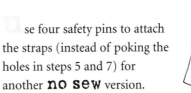

Use four safety pins to attach the straps (instead of poking the holes in steps 5 and 7) for another **no sew** version.

Cut three more strips off the bottom of the shirt to make two straps of the same color—it'll shorten step 3, and shorten the shirt.

all strung out

Sometimes sexy is simple. With a single panel of fabric across the front and mere strings holding it on, this tank is essentially a cloth breastplate that lets you play serious peekaboo with your back. (You better be ready to lose the bra, though, because otherwise it's going to look tacky. And tacky just doesn't go with sexy.)

LEVEL 1

---

ingredients

- 1 T-shirt (L or XL)
- ruler
- tailor's chalk
- scissors

Lay the T-shirt flat and cut a rectangle at least 16" long and at least 18" wide across the front of the shirt. Cut a tube from the bottom of the shirt. Reserve the rectangle.

Starting at the top of the tube, cut one long, continuous 1"-wide strip by spiraling around until you reach the bottom, as shown. Cut this strip in half to make two equal 1" strips.

Poke a hole in both upper corners of the rectangle, 1" from the top and side edges. Again, 1" from the edge, poke two more small holes along each side of the rectangle, 5" and 10" below the first.

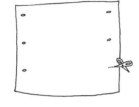

Tie a knot at the end of each strip. Lay the rectangle wrong side up and thread one strip through one of the top holes (from right side to wrong side). Thread the other strip through the opposite hole. Pull both strips through gently until the knots fit snugly against the fabric.

(back)

Cross the strips and lace them through the holes on the opposite sides as you would a shoe, until you reach the bottom.

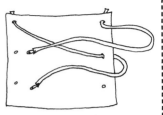

(back)

Slip it over your head, sliding your arms between the laces of the first and second holes, as indicated. The front of the tank top will gently drape, giving a slight cowl effect. Adjust the lacing as necessary for tightness. Then tie a bow.

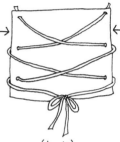

(back)

variation

ame concept, different execution. Cut a pentagon from the bottom hem and snip small holes at the side points. Thread a drawstring through the hem of the shirt (now the neckline), cross the ends, and lace them through the side holes. Tie them in a bow.

tying game

My little sister, always on the lookout for unusual tees, once woke me up at three A.M. to describe the must-have tank top she saw a girl wearing outside a crowded club. After listening to her breathless, slightly incoherent description—"all the knots down her back . . . like a horse's mane . . . or a stegosaurus"— I turned on the light and fumbled to sketch it. After a good night's sleep, the dream tank took me only 10 minutes to make. **LEVEL 1.5**

ingredients

1 T-shirt (L or XL)
scissors
ruler

1 Lay the T-shirt flat, cut off the sleeves just inside the seams, cut out the neck band just below the seam. Cut off the bottom 2" of the shirt through both layers.

2 Widen the neckline by cutting (through both layers of fabric) along the base of the neckline, leaving at least 2" for a shoulder strap. (The result should be a shallow boatneck.)

Flip the T-shirt over and cut straight up the center (through the back layer only), from the bottom to the neckline.

(back)

Into each side of the two new edges, cut horizontal slits about 3" into the edge and 1" to 1 ½" apart, creating strips all the way down the back of the shirt.

(back)

Starting at the top, tie the right and left strips together in a knot. Continue down the back until the bottom two strips have been knotted together.

(back)

Try the shirt on, knots in the back (sort of a stegosaurus-chic going on, with the ends of the knots looking like plates down the back), and arrange the straps for a little off-the-shoulder action.

variations

ather the tops of the straps with a few punk pins, or cut a small strip from the piece of fabric you chopped off the bottom in step 1 to tie a small bow around the top of one or both straps.

or a tighter fit, cut longer slits in step 4. (The knots will have a more dangly effect.)

ear the tank backward and pinch the shoulder straps together with a safety pin for this halter look, right.

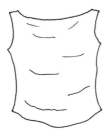

punk'd

An asymmetrical cut with flirty, carnival-esque punk pins placed just so, this tank is fun to make and just as fun to wear. It's loud, proud, and punked out. Just like you.

LEVEL 2

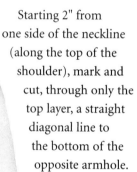

ingredients

1 T-shirt (S or M)

scissors

tailor's chalk

T-shirt scraps

5 punk pins

Lay the T-shirt flat. Cut out the neck band and cut off the sleeves just inside the seams.

Starting 2" from one side of the neckline (along the top of the shoulder), mark and cut, through only the top layer, a straight diagonal line to the bottom of the opposite armhole.

Turn the shirt over and make the same cut along the back, connecting to the ends of the cut you made in step 2.

(back)

From the T-shirt scraps, cut four 1"-wide strips, each at least 28" long, and pin the ends together. Then pin the bundle of strips to the back of the tank, on the side opposite the existing strap.

(back)

Use the four punk pins to pin each of the dangling ends at one of the four dots. Try on the tank top and adjust the length of the strips.

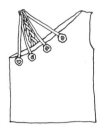

Pair two of the four strips together and braid them with the other two strips, making a 10" braided rope. (It will go up to your shoulder.) Let the ends dangle.

About 1" in from the front neckline edge, mark four small dots, evenly spaced, along the neckline, ending at the center, as shown.

variations

nstead of using punk pins, poke holes, thread the strips through, and make knots to secure them back and front. Knot bad, knot bad at all.

celebri-tee corner

Kickin' It: A model of good behavior, **Christy Turlington** kicked her own bad habit, then kicked off her "Smoking is Ugly" campaign with a sexy one-strap tank as her billboard. (It's a version of Punk'd, without the straps.)

f the plain single-strap tank top stretches out around your bust and you're feeling a little modest, grab a ribbon, snip small holes about 2" apart around the perimeter of the top opening of the shirt, and thread the ribbon in and out through alternating holes.

strip search

G et horizontal. Who says vertical stripes are the only way to go? This design breaks the rules and does it with style. Try black-and-white tees for prison stripes, or add a few colored T-shirts to your palette for multihue magic. The bow on one shoulder finishes it off with a flourish.

LEVEL 5

---

ingredients

---

2 T-shirts (L or XL, in different colors)

measuring tape

tailor's chalk

scissors

straight pins

needle

thread

Lay both T-shirts flat. Trim off the bottom hems, and cut three 5"-wide loops off the bottom of one shirt and two 5"-wide loops off the bottom of the second shirt.

Cut through one side of each loop to make five long strips. Cut four of the strips to a length that equals your bust measurement plus 1" (x).

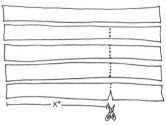

Lay out the strips in alternating colors, with the longest on top.

4 Lay the bottom two strips on top of each other, right sides together. Pin along the top edge. Repeat with the next two strips.

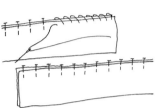

5 About ¼" from the edge, sew along both pinned edges with a whipstitch. Remove pins.

6 Place the two sewn panels together, right sides facing in, and pin along the top edge. (*Note:* Be sure the colors of your strips are still alternating.)

7 About ¼" from the edge, sew along the pinned edges with a whipstitch. Remove pins. (*Note:* The whole panel should be about 17" high.)

8 Center the fifth strip along one edge of the panel, right sides together, so there is an equal amount of fabric on each side. Pin along the edge.

9 Using a whipstitch, sew along the pinned edge as you did in steps 5 and 7, this time stopping 4" shy of the sides of the panel, as shown. Remove pins.

10 Fold the entire panel in half vertically, right sides together. Pin along the edges of the four bottom strips and sew using a whipstitch. (This will be your side seam.)

11 Remove the pins, turn the tank top right side out, and slip your torso through the tube. Tie the ends of the fifth strip over your shoulder.

variation

1 Leave all five strips long in step 2. Stitch together with enough length unsewn at the ends so you can tie them around you as a tube top.

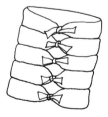

turn on the tube

14 tube tops (and halters, too!)— even *less* shirt, even *more* style. (With less coverage, it's a good time to review your drawstring technique.)

The doctor is in. And she's performing major reconstructive surgery. If you haven't noticed yet, the shirts in this book keep getting smaller and smaller. That's what happens when you give a girl some scissors. Tube tops, halter tops, the bandeau, and the bikini—we're getting to the good stuff now, for a no-holds-barred sexy summer. In this chapter, shoulders will be revealed and abs laid bare. Even those usually hidden spots—your lower back, the tops of your breasts—will get some exposure. So break out the sunscreen. (Doctor's orders.)

In the realm of feminine fashion, the tube top is an anomaly, bridging the gap between teen dance club trends and walking-down-the-aisle elegance. The sleeveless, strapless style is flirty, revealing, and, as long as we call the top of that wedding dress a "bodice," it's fit to wear in churches everywhere. The halter top also crosses the divide between casual and couture. Both styles embrace exposed shoulders and highlight the collarbones, a uniquely feminine part of the body. "More than pretty," goes the description in an Updike story, "this clean bare plane of the top of her chest down from the shoulder bones like a dented sheet of metal tilted in the light . . ."

But let's talk comfort, too. When it's 85° outside and you want to be allowed in the supermarket, the halter or tube top is like a second skin. With both halters and tubes, you ditch the bra entirely (or wear a strapless one). You're really stretching your resources with this style, leaving enough fabric for another project—a hat, a wristband, maybe even matching gauntlets.

The tube top is basic, but it doesn't have to be boring. Think creatively about how to modify your T-shirts' preexisting graphics, patterns, and letters—by adding or subtracting, turning them on their side or upside down, you can transform an otherwise questionable design into abstract expressionism. Because the projects in this chapter are *so* deconstructed, you really don't need a top-of-the-line T-shirt to pull them off. Aggressive refashioning can give the lamest tee in the bunch its day in the sun.

So don't be afraid to go against the grain. Even the cotton industry folks who bring us T-shirts get a little subversive in their ad campaigns: "Fashion Rule #1: Ignore Fashion Rules."

Rocker Gwen Stefani throws down the gauntlet for self-made fashion.

boob tube

imple fact: Breasts are probably the most fascinating part of the female anatomy. The old poets sang their praises. Construction workers whistle at the sight of them. And tube tops were made to show them off. This basic tube is a year-round staple—bare it all in the summer months and cover up with a cardigan or hoodie when it gets chilly. The shape of the tube is pretty straightforward, so spice it up by using one of your more wildly patterned T-shirts. **LEVEL 3**

---

ingredients
---

1 T-shirt
(preferably fitted)

scissors

straight pins

needle

thread

1 scrap drawstring

Turn the T-shirt inside out and cut off both sleeves just inside the seams. Cut off the top of the shirt just below the neckline, through both layers.

Cut along each side of the shirt just inside the armholes to make two straight-edged rectangles.

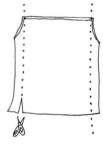

Pin the front and back along both sides and sew, using a whipstitch.

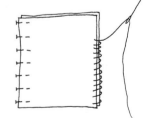

Fold the top edge down 1" around the circumference of the tube. Pin and sew using a running stitch.

Turn right side out. At the center front, make two small incisions in the top layer of the fold about 1" apart. Run the drawstring (cut from another T-shirt) through one hole and out the other.

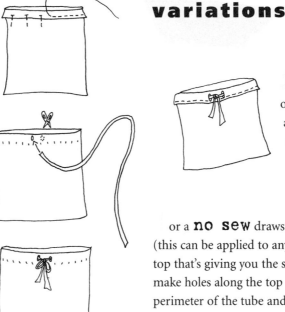

Slip your tube top on and tie the drawstring in a bow.

variations

old the fabric out instead of in at step 4 and sew, for a more visible drawstring casing.

or a **no sew** drawstring (this can be applied to any tube top that's giving you the slip), make holes along the top perimeter of the tube and thread a strip of fabric in and out of the holes for a quick-fix cinch.

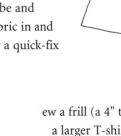

ew a frill (a 4" tube from a larger T-shirt) to the top or bottom of the tube top. (See project 58, Skirt Flirt, for instructions on how to make the ruffle.)

tees in the movies

Forrest Gump (1994) Celebrated (along with the rest of pop culture) the smiley face T-shirt! Off the silver screen, a small advertising agency in Massachusetts was said to have introduced the smiling yellow circle in 1963. Today it graces T-shirts, buttons, posters, and e-mail emoticons.

bodice snipper

amilla trembled. It was finally happening.

"You're all I ever wanted," Brett whispered, his voice a low growl as he lunged for her. "Why, your bodice is already ripped!" he gasped, certain she loved another.

"Not ripped, snipped," she quipped. Her lily-white cheeks flushed deep crimson as she recalled the night of passionate refashioning. "I made the bodice myself, from a T-shirt I once loved. I cut it at the top, to make room for my ample bosom."

His eyes blazed with jealousy. "I won't compete with a piece of cloth, Camilla—I can't."

"Brett, don't. That's all over now. . . . I only have eyes for you," she swore, fingers crossed behind her back.

Turn the T-shirt inside out and lay it flat. Cut through both layers from the bottom of one sleeve across to the bottom of the other.

ingredients

1 T-shirt
(M, L, or XL)
tailor's chalk
scissors
straight pins
measuring tape
needle
thread

2 Divide your bust measurement by 2 and then, beginning at one side, measure and mark that length (x) along the T-shirt hem. (*Note:* The hem will become the top of your tube.) Mark a line from top to bottom at that measurement and cut along it through both layers, removing the excess fabric.

3 Pin along the edge you just cut and sew it together using a whipstitch. Remove the pins and turn the tube right side out. Rotate the tube top so that the seam you made is centered in the back, and the original T-shirt hem is at the top.

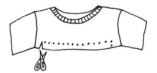

4 Cut a strip 1" wide and 14" to 16" long from the T-shirt scraps to use as a drawstring.

5 At the center front of the shirt, starting ½" from the top edge, snip or poke 10 small holes—five ½" to the left of the center point and five ½" to the right—spaced 1" apart, as shown.

6 Starting at the top, thread the drawstring through one of the holes (outside to inside). Pull it up through the hole below it and down through the next.

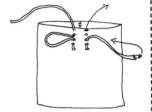

7 At the bottom hole, run the string over to the other line of five holes and continue "sewing" in and out until you reach the top.

8 Try the tube on and pull the two drawstrings to cinch the bust. Tie a cute little bow—let the ends dangle or tuck them inside.

variations

1 Leave the tube top as is after step 3 for the classic fitted go-to tank. Layer it under project 44, Knotty by Nature.

2 For a **no sew** version, use a small (I mean *really* fitted) tightly knit shirt, cut a straight line across from underarm to underarm, and follow the directions for the cinch.

ready-made

It's like a magic trick. Hold up an extra-large tee and tell your friends that it's your favorite refashioned shirt. *But that's just a big ugly T-shirt,* they'll think, convinced you've lost all sense of style. Then, disappear behind door #1, shirt in hand, and emerge moments later wearing Ready-Made. One of the simplest tubes to make, it's also one of the hottest. A lazy girl's favorite, it involves no sewing, measuring, or even cutting. All you need to remember is one of those knots you learned back in summer camp. **LEVEL 1**

---

ingredient

---

1 T-shirt (XL)

Arms up! Let the shirt slide down as you stick your arms and shoulders through the neck hole.

Rotate the T-shirt around your torso so that the back of the shirt is in front.

Tie the sleeves together over your chest in a double (square) knot. (A granny knot won't hold.) Tie the bottom two corners of the shirt together in a double knot at your waist.

(back)

Rotate the tube so that both knots are bustled in the back. Like magic!

tees in the movies

Breathless (1960): When she appeared in the cult classic with "Herald Tribune" emblazoned across her chest, actress Jean Seberg was the first girl to wear a T-shirt onscreen. Until the 1960s, the T-shirt was exclusively a male article of clothing.

variation

kip the second half of step 3 and leave the bottom untied—it's a very cute option to wear with jeans. When shorter gals wear this variation, it can actually pass as a dress!

bow me over

I love this one so much, I made it twice in one sitting (one in New York Liberty orange, and one in skull-and-crossbones black). The bow keeps the tube from falling down *and* gives you the sexiest back, proving once and for all that function and style go hand in hand. Function, meet style. Style, meet function. Get comfortable—you two are going to be spending a lot of time together. **LEVEL 3**

---

ingredients

---

2 T-shirts
(at least 1 L or XL)
measuring tape
tailor's chalk
scissors
needle
thread

Lay one of the T-shirts flat on the floor and cut across the shirt 10" from the bottom through both layers of fabric. Snip through the back of the loop so you have a long 10"-wide strip.

Lay the strip flat. With chalk, mark the lengthwise center of the strip. Measure around your torso and mark the measurement (x) along the long edge of the fabric so that it is centered (with an equal amount of fabric on each side of the initial chalk mark). This keeps the design on the T-shirt centered. Mark and cut off any excess fabric. Put the strip aside.

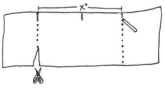

Lay the second (L or XL) T-shirt flat and cut a 6"-wide strip from the bottom through both layers of fabric.

Snip through the side of the loop so you have a long 6"-wide strip.

Center the 6" strip on top of the 10" panel right sides together (so the bottom edge of the 6" panel lines up with the top edge of the 10" panel). Pin along that shared edge.

Divide the number you calculated in step 2 by 2. Center that measurement along the pinned edge and mark the two end points with chalk.

Using a backstitch, *sew only between the chalk marks* along the pinned edge, leaving a ½" seam allowance. (Example: If your 10" panel is 40" long, sew only the 20" at the center so there are 10" unsewn on either side.)

Remove the pins and lay the now-connected panels flat.

Fold the piece in half lengthwise, wrong side out, lining up the vertical edges of the bottom strip, as shown. Pin along the edges and sew using a whipstitch. Remove pins.

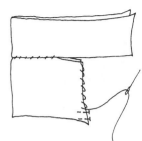

Turn right side out. Slip the tube on and tie the loose ends of the top panel in the back.

(back)

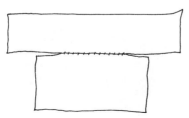

More Janis Joplin than Jane Austen, here's an Empire waist that not only gets you in the club, but gets you a backstage pass as well. Wear this streamlined tube with your chunkiest jewelry (big earrings, heavy pendant) as you sing, dance, scream, and sweat. The slanted edge puts the spotlight on your hips as you're swept into the fray. **LEVEL 3**

ingredients

1 T-shirt (L or XL)
scissors
measuring tape
tailor's chalk
straight pins
needle
thread

Turn the T-shirt inside out and lay it flat. Cut off the sleeves just inside the seams. Cut in a straight line through both layers across the top of the shirt just below the neck band.

Divide your bust measurement by 2 (x). Center this length along the top edge of the shirt, and mark with chalk.

Between the chalk marks, measure, mark, and cut a rectangle 6" to 7" high through both layers. Pin the short edges of the rectangles together and sew using a whipstitch ¼" from the edge. Remove the pins and set this tube aside.

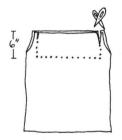

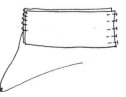

Center and mark the same measurement (x) along the top of the shirt. Draw lines from the two marks to the bottom corners of the shirt and cut along them.

Pin closed the edges you cut in step 4 and mark a diagonal line from one bottom corner to a point 3" to 4" up on the opposite side. Cut along that line through both layers.

Sew the pinned edges with a whipstitch ¼" from the edge, leaving a 3" to 4" slit open on the longer side. Remove the pins and turn the tube right side out.

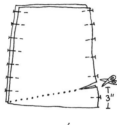

Place the first tube around the top of this tube, right sides together, making sure the side seams line up. Pin around the top edge.

Using a whipstitch or zigzag stitch, sew along the pinned edge.

Remove the pins, turn up the top tube, wear it out and live it up.

variations

ake Natural Sass for your ass (in other words, make it a little wider and wear it as a skirt). Or, try project 63, Mud Flap.

o totally classic and "totally tubular," right. Make two traditionally shaped tubes and sew them together as you did in step 7.

scarf ace

For a sophisticated evening look, choose the tube top with built-in elegance. An added drape of fabric creates a sensual line as it wraps across your breasts, around your neck, and down your back, swaying gently as you pass. When the fashion photogs hound you on the red carpet about who you're wearing, you can purr, "I'm wearing a _____ original.

(insert your name here)

LEVEL 4

ingredients

2 T-shirts
measuring tape
tailor's chalk
scissors
straight pins
needle
thread

Lay one of the T-shirts flat and remove the bottom hem just above the stitching. Then cut an 8" strip off the bottom of the shirt through both layers. Snip through the side of the loop so you have an 8"-long panel of fabric. Set it aside.

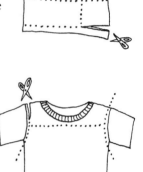

Turn the second T-shirt inside out and lay it flat. Cut off both sleeves just inside the seams. Then mark and cut a straight line across the top of the shirt just below the neckline.

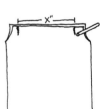

Divide your bust measurement by 2 (x). Center this measurement along the top edge of the shirt and mark with chalk.

Between the chalk marks, measure, mark, and cut a rectangle 6" to 7" high through both layers.

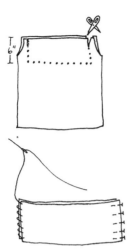

Pin the short edges of the rectangles together on each side and sew with a whipstitch. Remove the pins and set the tube aside.

Center and mark the measurement (x) from step 3 across the top of the second T-shirt. From those marks, measure about 10" down from the top edge to form a rectangle. Cut out the rectangle through both layers.

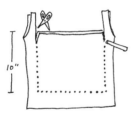

Pin along the vertical edges, and sew them together with a whipstitch. Remove the pins and turn the tube right side out.

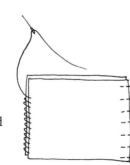

Now take the 8" strip you cut in step 1 and, with right sides together, place one end against the front of the 10" tube, centering it between the side seams. Pin it in place.

Take the 6" to 7" tube made in step 5 (still inside out) and place it (with right sides together) around the circumference of the top of the 10" tube, lining up the seams on each side (the end of the 8" strip will be sandwiched in between). Pin the edges, making sure to go through all three layers in the front.

Using a whipstitch, sew around the pinned edge. Remove the pins.

Try on the tube (the 6" to 7" panel should cover your chest) and wrap the 8" strip around your neck once like a scarf, letting it dangle down the back.

rollover

Cell phone companies keep promising me rollover minutes. My yoga teacher tells me to roll over on the mat. I order sushi rolls over and over again. Here's one of those times when life imitates art. Wear this design to a gallery opening or outdoor film festival—the off-the-shoulder rollover top is off the hook.

ingredients

- 1 T-shirt (L or XL)
- measuring tape
- scissors
- tailor's chalk
- straight pins
- needle
- thread

Lay the T-shirt flat and cut an 8"-wide loop off the bottom of the shirt. Set it aside.

Measure and mark 12" from the new bottom of the shirt. Cut horizontally across at that mark through both layers of fabric. Then snip through the side of the loop, creating a long rectangular strip.

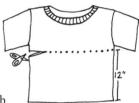

Lay the strip flat and mark a length equal to your bust measurement (x) along the long edge of the rectangle. Cut vertically to remove the excess fabric.

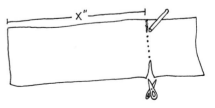

4 Fold the rectangle in half lengthwise, right sides together. Pin along the short ends and sew the edge with a whipstitch.

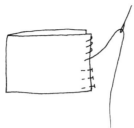

5 Remove the pins. Turn the resulting 12"-high tube right side out and lay it flat. Turn the loop from step 1 inside out and center it above the 12" tube so that its bottom (cut) edge meets the 12" tube's top edge.

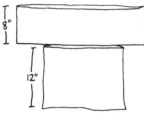

6 From both sides of the 12" tube, measure 2½" in and mark with chalk. Pin the tubes together between the two marked points and sew along the pinned edge using a whipstitch. Remove the pins.

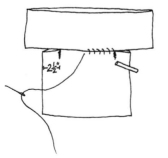

7 Flip the shirt over and repeat step 6 on the back.

8 Try the shirt on and roll the top tube over 4" to 5" so the right side of the fabric is facing out. Rollover is complete.

variations

Play the tying game: Make the top rollover piece extra long, snip through it to make a strip, and tie the ends together in a bow in the front or back.

Make the two pieces of the top out of two different T-shirts.

Use punk pins or a brooch or snap-on hair clips to add some bunching to your rollover.

bandeau, james bandeau

This bandeau has serious retro sex appeal. It's got style. It's got class. Agent 007 never went incognito—and with this little number, you won't, either. (And it's meaningless to speak of "undercover" when there's so little covering you.) Feeling dangerous?

LEVEL 2

---

ingredients

- 1 T-shirt
- ruler
- tailor's chalk
- scissors

1 Lay the T-shirt flat and cut off the hem just above the stitching. Then cut a 6" to 8"-wide (10" to 12" for the better endowed) strip off the bottom of the shirt through both layers. Snip through the side of the loop so you have a long strip.

2 From the remaining T-shirt, mark and cut a smaller strip about 10" long and 3" wide. Lay the small strip flat, wrong side up.

"The T-shirt has always been an icon of freedom."
—Dov Charney, American Apparel CEO

Lay the large strip (also wrong side up) on top of the small one so it is centered over and perpendicular to the small strip (creating the shape of a cross).

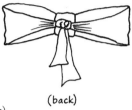

With the knot centered at your chest, wrap the large strip of fabric around your bust and tie another (tighter) knot in the back. Ta da! Short and sweet (in more ways than one).

(back)

Gently but securely, double-knot the smaller strip around the larger one. (Don't pull the first knot so tight that the bandeau bunches completely.)

variations

or an even simpler **no sew** project, simply tie the 6" strip around you and go!

ix it up by using a different T-shirt fabric for the middle strip.

tees in the movies

The Deep (1977): The wet T-shirt contest is often traced back to a scene in this movie when a clothed Jacqueline Bisset swam underwater and resurfaced in her sexy wet tee.

nstead of a piece of fabric, use a safety pin or punk pin to bunch the fabric in the middle.

ew the tube of the bandeau closed in the front and cover it with the small tie.

knotty by nature

It's macramé for club kids. Layer this tease of a top over a plain tube or bandeau for a daring night out. Whether the scene is rowdy house music or seductive gypsy ballads, these knotty tassels are with you at every turn, practically doing the flirting for you. **LEVEL 3**

ingredients

- 1 T-shirt (L or XL)
- scissors
- measuring tape
- tailor's chalk
- needle
- thread

Turn the T-shirt inside out and lay it flat. Cut off the sleeves just inside the seams. Cut straight across the shirt, through both layers, just below the neck band.

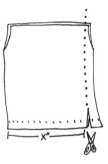

Divide your bust measurement by 2 and measure and mark that length (x) along the bottom edge. (*Note:* The hem will become the top of your tube.) Starting at the chalk mark, draw a vertical line to the top. Cut along the line through both layers.

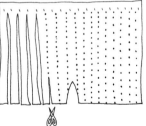

Lay the piece of fabric flat, wrong side up, with the hem at the top, and use a ruler and chalk to mark an even number of 1"-wide strips for fringe. Leaving a 2" margin at the top, cut these strips from the bottom of the tube up (it's okay if they're different lengths).

Fold the piece in half length-wise and use a whipstitch to sew only the top 2" of the sides back together again, as shown.

This step is easier to do if you're wearing the tube, so slip it on over a tank top. Pair off each of the dangling strips and tie them loosely in double knots. Rotate the shirt around your torso as you go.

When you get back to the first knot, take one of its dangling strips and one from the second knot, and tie them together. Continue around the shirt until an entire second row of knots has been made.

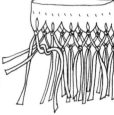

On the third row, pair the same strips that made the knots in the first row. Continue in the same fashion, making fourth and fifth rows for as long as you have strips to tie.

Trim the ends if you want them to be even. Wear this flirty shirt over a bandeau or other tube top and give me your best shimmy.

halt right there

Transitions can be hard. Puberty. Leaving college for the real world. Starting a new job. This project is one of the most painless transitions you'll make—from tube top to halter top. Take your basic tube, add a strap or two, and tie. See? *So* not a big deal. For added incentive: The straight lines of the halter design accentuate your curves (one of the great rewards of making it through that first big transition).

LEVEL 1

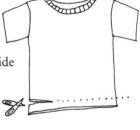

Lay the T-shirt flat and cut a strip ½" to 1" wide off the bottom of the shirt. Set it aside to become your halter tie.

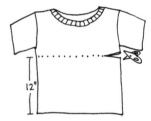

Measure and mark with chalk 12" up from the bottom of the shirt and cut across the T-shirt through both layers of fabric, creating a tube.

At the center front of the tube, snip or poke two holes 8" apart and 1" from the top edge.

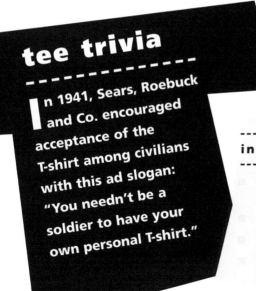

tee trivia

In 1941, Sears, Roebuck and Co. encouraged acceptance of the T-shirt among civilians with this ad slogan: "You needn't be a soldier to have your own personal T-shirt."

---

ingredients

- 1 T-shirt (relatively fitted)
- scissors
- ruler
- chalk

Thread the strip you created in step 1 into one of the holes, from outside to inside, and then out through the adjacent hole. Pull the strip of fabric until it is centered in the tube.

Put on the halter and tie the straps in a bow behind your neck.

variations

or more **no sew** fun, poke holes through both the front and back sides in step 3, thread a string through each hole, and tie the ends over your shoulders as tank top straps.

dd layers of fringe to the halter for a flapper top (see project 72, Flapper Frenzy, for the technique—as well as the full dress).

cover girl

Three words: Easy. Breezy. Beautiful. This one made the cover of the book, and it's not hard to see why. The low-cut halter looks attractive on the large- and small-breasted alike, and the knot in the back crops the top conveniently to reveal that tattoo on your lower back. If Marilyn Monroe had been a hipster, this is what she would have worn.

LEVEL 4

ingredients

- 1 T-shirt (L)
- ruler
- scissors
- tailor's chalk
- needle
- thread
- straight pins

Lay the T-shirt flat and cut 12" off the bottom, leaving the hem.

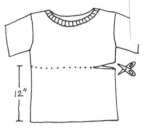

With chalk, mark a 12"-long teardrop shape about 9" wide at the bottom and 3" wide at one shoulder, as shown. Cut out through both layers of fabric, keeping the shoulder seam, which becomes the center back of the halter piece.

Using a basting stitch, sew along the bottom of each end of the halter piece.

Gather the fabric at the bottom of each end along the stitched area, reducing its length from 9" to 6".

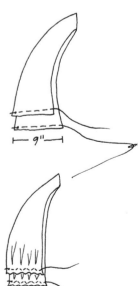

Leaving about 1" between them, pin the two gathered ends at the center of the hem edge of the 12" tube (right sides together).

Using a whipstitch, sew along the pinned edges to complete the halter. Remove the pins and basting stitches.

At the center back, make a vertical cut through the tube to create two tying ends.

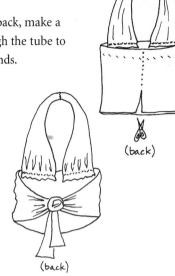

(back)

Slip the halter over your head and tie the two ends together at your back.

(back)

celebri-tee corner

variations

ake the halter piece and the torso piece out of contrasting T-shirts.

nstead of gathering the tube ends in a knot at the back, sew them together in a straight, flat seam. And, instead of slipping the halter over your head, use two gathered rectangular pieces (then follow steps 3 through 6) and tie them at your neck. Very Studio 54.

t-bird

Seventies clothes are crazy fun, but let's be honest—polyester can get itchy and trap unsavory B.O. With this high-necked halter, you're combining that '70s shape with a more breathable fabric. Ah, cotton—the fabric of our lives. **LEVEL 3**

Turn the T-shirt inside out, lay it flat, and cut off the sleeves just inside the seams. Cut a 1" strip off the bottom to use later as a drawstring.

Note: If the T-shirt is much too wide for you, now is the time to clip a little off the sides and resew the seams farther in—see the Classic Punk tank top, project 14, as a guide.

ingredients

1 T-shirt
scissors
ruler
tailor's chalk
straight pins
needle
thread

On the front, cut slight diagonal lines from the base of each armhole to the top of the shoulder (about 3" to the left and right of the neck band), as shown. Then cut a straight line across the top, through both layers

On the back, mark and cut (through only the back layer) a gentle arc from the bottom of one armhole to the bottom of the other. Remove the excess fabric.

(back)

Flip the shirt over and fold the top edge down 1½" against the front of the shirt. Pin in place.

Using a running stitch or backstitch, sew along the pinned area 1" from the folded edge. Remove pins.

Thread the drawstring through the casing completed in step 5, and bunch the fabric around it.

Turn the halter right-side out, try it on, and tie the drawstring ends at the back of your neck. (You can tie a small knot at each end of the string to keep it from slipping out of the casing.)

variation

You can make this project a **no sew** by using the original bottom hem (on a smaller T-shirt) as the drawstring casing at the top of your halter. Cut a straight line from the bottom of one sleeve to the bottom of the other. Flip the shirt upside down and cut an arc out of the back. In the front, leaving at least 8" of hem in the middle, cut diagonal lines to meet the arc. Thread a drawstring through what's left of the hem and tie it on!

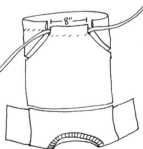

twisted sister

I walked out of work one day and nearly collided with a girl wearing this ingenious halter. It was as if the T-shirt reconstruction gods had sent her. Excited to add the design to my style palette, I chased her down the street to find out how she had made it. Though she was quite content to keep her headphones on and volume cranked up, I'm glad, for your sake, that she took the time to spill the beans on her DIY creation. The twisted neck turned out to be far easier to make than I had expected!

LEVEL 1

tee trivia

Heavy-duty: A 1,000-acre cotton farm can produce enough cotton (about 500,000 pounds!) to make more than 1 million T-shirts.

ingredients

1 T-shirt (M)
scissors
tailor's chalk
4 small safety pins

Lay the T-shirt flat and cut off the sleeves just inside the seams.

Flip the shirt over. From the base of one armhole, mark and cut a gentle arc across *only the back* of the shirt to the base of the other armhole. (You'll have a bib-like flap at the back of the shirt.)

(back)

Tuck the back flap up through the neck hole (from the inside of the shirt, out) so that it twists slightly. Continue wrapping the fabric around the neck band until the entire neckline is bunchy and twisted.

(*Note:* It's helpful to be wearing the shirt at this stage so you can tell how many twists you need.)

(back)

Use four small safety pins to tack the twists in place (so you don't have to retwist every time you put on the halter top). Pin from the inside so the pins are not visible on the outside.

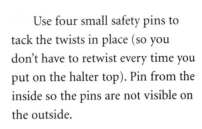

variations

ake a vertical cut up the center of the back flap through the neck band and twist and tie the two ends together at the nape of your neck.

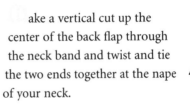

nstead of safety pins, use a few stitches to tack the twists in place.

celebri-tee corner

No wardrobe malfunction here—it was a wardrobe reconstruction at this halftime show. During the 2004–05 season, the **New Jersey Nets cheerleaders** performed dances in refashioned (yes, sexy) halter tops made from T-shirts bearing their team's logo.

teeny bikini

This T-shirt bikini is nearly one-size-fits-all. But you can add an inch to each measurement to make it one size bigger. By the way, those aren't just triangles covering your bubbies; they arc at the bottom so that when they're bunched they have more dimension.

Note: Teeny Bikini is double-lined to prevent the wet T-shirt contest look. I wouldn't advise surfing in it, but wading and sunbathing are just fine. **LEVEL 5**

---
ingredients
---

1 T-shirt (XL)

T-shirt scraps cut into 1"-wide strips:
1 strip 48" long,
2 strips 24" long,
4 strips 16" long

ruler

tailor's chalk

scissors

straight pins

needle

thread

Bikini top: If you anticipate losing steam during this time-consuming project, make the top first—it's the more versatile piece.

Lay the T-shirt flat, cut off the hem just above the stitching, and then cut 9" off the bottom through both layers.

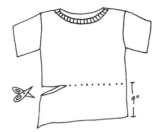

Pin the two layers together to keep them from shifting. With chalk, draw two triangular shapes on the folded fabric, about 8" on two sides and 10" along the base, with an arc measuring 1" at the farthest point from the base. (After hemming, these shapes will measure about 6" by 6" by 8".) *Note:* If you prefer, make a paper pattern first.

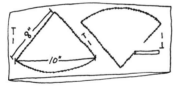

Cut along the marked lines, making sure to go through both layers. You should have two double-layer shapes (from here on out, consider them as one piece of fabric, where the back of the T-shirt is the "wrong" side of the fabric).

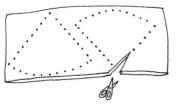

Wrong side up, fold down the top point of one of the triangles about 1". Take the two 24" strips and stretch them out. Lay the end of one strip over the folded point of the triangle, overlapping 1", and pin. Repeat with the second triangle.

Fold over ½" along each of the 8" sides of the triangle, and pin. (*Note:* The foldovers should fit snugly around the strap.) Using a small backstitch, sew along the pinned areas, ¼" from the edge. Be sure to sew the straps securely to the peaks of the triangles. Remove pins.

continued

Fold over 1" along the bottom (arced) side of the triangle and pin in place.

Using a small backstitch, sew along the pinned area, ¾" from the edge (this forms the draw-string casing, big enough to draw the back ties through). Remove pins.

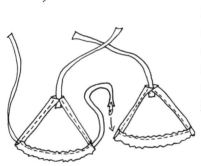

Thread the 48" strip through the bottom of both triangles, gathering the fabric slightly over the strip.

What are you waiting for? Try it on! Tie the top straps behind your neck and the bottom straps around your back. (You may now withdraw your membership at the topless beach.)

Bikini bottom:

There's no easy way to describe the shape of the bikini bottom; if you own a store-bought one, you can lay it on the fabric and trace it as a pattern, leaving an extra 1" margin all around. Or, you can snip the sides of an old pair of undies, lay them flat, and trace around them, leaving 1" seam allowances. But for the brave, here goes . . .
(*Note:* If there is a graphic on the front of the shirt, it will end up gracing your rear.)

From the rest of the T-shirt, measure, mark, and cut (through both layers of fabric) a vertical rectangle 16" wide and 19" high.

With chalk, sketch wide arcs from the top corners to the bottom corners of the rectangles, creating a sort of hourglass shape, as shown. The narrowest part

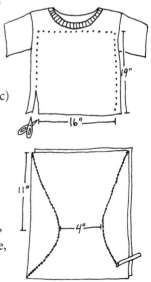

should measure 4" across and fall about 11" down from the top of the rectangle. *Note:* If you prefer, make a paper pattern first.

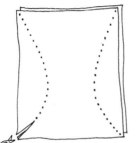

Cut along the arcs through both layers of fabric and flip them over as a unit, so the back side of the shirt is facing up.

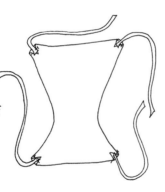

Fold over the point of each corner about 1" and pin. Lay the end of one of the four 16" strips at each of the four corners and pin them in place with 1" of overlap.

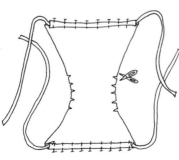

Fold over 1" along the top and bottom edges and pin. Make five ¼" snips along both sides of the narrowest part of the hourglass, to help the fabric "give" when making the seam.

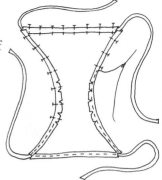

Carefully fold over ½" of fabric along the arced edges and pin in place. Make sure the strips are well tucked into each corner.

Using a backstitch, sew along the pinned areas ¼" from the folded edge. Remove pins.

Try the bottom on your bottom, tightly tying the strings in bows at your hips. *Optional:* Tie small knots at the ends of the four strings.

variation

atch the bikini bottom to any of the halter or tank tops in the book, and you've got a tankini.

skirting the issue

Introducing 23 projects that take the T-shirt downtown—and we're not talking about the financial district in New York City.

Remember games of make-believe when draping a T-shirt over your head was enough to turn you into a princess with long, flowing hair? Though you couldn't get a comb through it, your hair was just beautiful and came in as many colors and patterns as you had T-shirts in your dresser. Kudos to your inventiveness, my jersey-knit Rapunzel. Tap into that childhood ingenuity and don't worry about where a T-shirt "belongs." Enter the world of T-*skirts*.

First women fought hard for the right to wear pants. Then we realized it was really all the clutter under our skirts—the girdles, the hoops, the whole wiry mess—that we hated. Skirts themselves are playful, liberating . . . just ask the kilt wearers of the world. Skirts inspire dancing and twirling. By comparison, pants seem much more restricted by style, length, and shape. And there are just so many *kinds* of skirts. Goth skirts with straps, clips, safety pins, and zippers. Princess skirts of chiffon and tulle. Librarian skirts with a very proper A-line. Superwoman super miniskirts, poised and ready for a mission. And if not being able to sit cross-legged on the floor is the only thing holding you back, wear pants underneath!

Why a T-shirt skirt? Jersey fabric hugs in just the right places—think what a finely knit, fitted T-shirt does for your breasts and apply that thought to your booty. T-shirt skirts are the comfiest, sexiest, swankiest skirts in town. They're soft and lightweight, and you get to choose from infinite styles and colors. If the T-shirts you refashion feature lots of colors and logos, wear the skirt with a white ribbed tank or a plain black top so the skirt becomes the centerpiece of your outfit.

If you're nervous about fashioning bottoms from items that usually go on top, don't be. Many of the skills you've practiced in the chapters on tanks and tube tops (like tying, cinching, and drawstrings) apply here. In fact, some of the T-skirts are multipurpose and can be worn as tubes, and vice versa.

With so many design choices, you can pick the skirt that matches who you feel like today—whether it's a party hostess, club crawler, or weekend athlete. Designer Donna Karan once said, "Fashion is all about creating an image. But the truth is, how a woman feels about herself sensually and spiritually comes from inside." It's time to let the inside girl show herself on the outside. So what are you waiting for? Let's play dress-up!

Never in fur, vegan Alicia Silverstone steps out in a skirt and halter made of T-shirt pelts.

snips ahoy

When a prism catches the light just right, it dazzles. Similarly, when you strike just the right pose, the hidden message in this skirt is brought to light. Think of it as your message in a bottle. Stencil a greeting, a picture, a pattern, or an SOS on the side of the skirt. Some ideas: a skull and crossbones, a heart, a comet, an anchor, the words "ROCK!" or "DORK," or your name or the name of your favorite team (Go Sox!). Use the point of your scissors to get your point across. **LEVEL 3**

Turn both T-shirts inside out and lay them flat. Cut straight across the front of each shirt just below the armholes to make two rectangular tubes of fabric. Trim off the hems of both tubes.

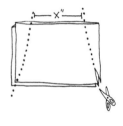

Divide your waist measurement by 2 (x). (Example: If your waist is 34", you'll be using a length of 17".) Layer the two tubes on top of each other and center the length x across the top. Mark both sides (left and right) of the measurement and draw diagonal lines

ingredients

- 2 T-shirts (L or XL, in different colors)
- scissors
- measuring tape
- tailor's chalk
- needle
- thread

from those marks to the bottom corners of the rectangle. Cut along those lines, through all four layers, creating a trapezoid shape.

Along the chalk lines, use a scissor point to poke (or snip) small holes, no larger than ¼", about ¾" apart.

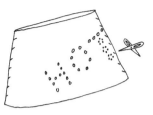

3 Separate the layers and pin the front and back of each shirt together along the angled edges of the two trapezoids. Cut 2" off the bottom of the T-shirt that you want to use as the outer layer.

When you've finished poking and snipping, insert the longer skirt inside the shorter one (right sides out and side seams aligned) and pin them together at the waist.

continued

4 Sew along the pinned edges using a whipstitch. Remove pins.

tees in the movies

5 Turn both skirts right side out. Take the shorter skirt and sketch the letters of a word (or image) you'd like to see on it.

The Wedding Singer (1998): **"Get out of my Van Halen T-shirt before you jinx the band and they break up!" —Robbie Hart (Adam Sandler) to his ex-girlfriend**

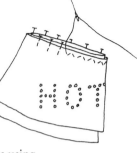

Use a zigzag stitch or a whipstitch to sew ¼" from the edge around the waist.

Optional: Tack the skirt layers in place by sewing through both skirts along the side seams using a running stitch.

Try on the skirt so that the color of the underskirt is revealed through the snipped holes in the overskirt.

variations

rainstorm more hidden message ideas and personalize skirts for your friends. Try a constellation (your astrological sign), Xs and Os, or zigzags.

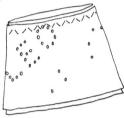

or an edgier look, cut the top skirt layer on an angle.

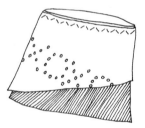

or a **no sew** version, use smaller shirts that hug your hips so you avoid having to sew up the sides. Along the waistbands of both skirts and starting 1" from the edge, make ¾"-deep vertical cuts about 3" apart. Thread a drawstring in and out of the holes (through both layers), binding the two skirts together, and tie the ends in a bow.

63

snip, crackle, pop!

The right combination of color and texture makes this classic shape all the more exciting. I decided to combine dark gray and orange. (It's as striking as black and orange, but not as Halloweeny.) Placing the dark panels at the sides is flattering on the hips, and their contrast with the orange makes the center panels pop. The slits and rough texture are simultaneously flirty and edgy. (If you're self-conscious about your thighs peeking through the slits, this skirt looks great over pants.) **LEVEL 3**

1 Lay both T-shirts flat. Measure 15" up from the bottom hems, mark, and cut horizontally across the torso of the shirts through both layers. You will have two 15" tubes (hems still attached). Set aside the tube you want to use for the side panels.

continued

ingredients

- 2 T-shirts (M, L, or XL)
- measuring tape
- tailor's chalk
- scissors (or razor blade)
- needle
- thread
- straight pins
- 1 flap from a cardboard box

Subtract 10" from your waist measurement and then divide by 2 (x). (Example: For a 35" waist, subtract 10 to get 25"; divide by 2 to get 12.5".) Center that measurement across the bottom of the first T-shirt tube and mark at each end. (This tube will become the front and back panels of your skirt.)

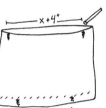

Add 4 to the measurement x and center it across the top edge of the tube and mark it at each end.

Draw a straight line connecting the two chalk marks on each side. Cut through both layers of fabric along the lines. (You'll have two matching trapezoids.) Set aside.

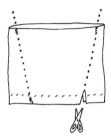

Take the second T-shirt tube and lay it flat. Mark and cut (through both layers) a smaller trapezoid that measures 5" at the hem and 10" at the top of the tube (it is, of course, already 15" high).

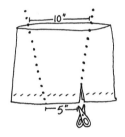

Pin the angled edges of the trapezoidal panels together (wrong sides together to create external seams), alternating the panels made from each shirt. (The hemmed edges will become the waistband of the skirt.)

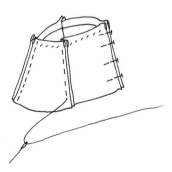

Sew the pinned edges ¼" from the edge using a running stitch. Remove pins.

Insert the cardboard flap between the layers of the skirt, to prevent you from cutting through more than one layer.

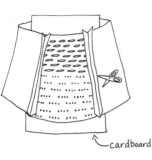

← cardboard

Using your ruler as a guide, cut 1"-wide horizontal slits about ½" apart across each of the side panels of the skirt. (*Note:* Don't get too close to the seams!)

Continue making slits in rows about 1" apart, staggering the slits slightly in each row like the pattern on a brick wall (see project 27, Heavy Meshinery) until you've completely filled the panel.

Repeat steps 9 and 10 on the other side panel. Slip the skirt on and go!

variations

dd a drawstring: When you're sewing the sides in step 7, leave 1" open at the waistband. Cut a strip from your scrap fabric and thread it through the waistband, tying the ends in a bow at your hip.

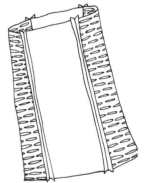

ake the panels long and narrow (try the full length of a T-shirt) for a more modest but equally edgy look.

kip the slitting and leave the side panels solid, as shown at left.

sidewinder

Have you ever seen a sidewinder snake on one of those National Geographic specials? It's mesmerizing to watch as it slithers and scoots across the sand, hugging the contours of the dunes. PBS-inspired, MTV-applicable, this skirt should fit snugly over your hips and thighs, making your every movement as slinky as a snake's and as beautiful to watch. **LEVEL 2**

----

ingredients

----

1 T-shirt (L or XL)
measuring tape
tailor's chalk
scissors

Lay the T-shirt flat, cut off the hem. Then cut two 1"-wide strips from the bottom of the shirt through both layers. Snip through the tubes, making them into long strips, and set aside.

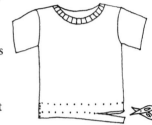

Divide your waist measurement by 2, and then subtract 1 (x). (Example: For a 36" waist, divide by 2 to get 18"; subtract 1 to get 17".) On the shirt front, mark and cut a rectangle 18" high by x" wide. (Be sure to cut through both layers.)

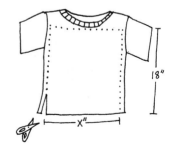

18"

x"

Using the point of one scissor blade, poke small holes (through both layers) about 1" apart and 1" from the side edges. Repeat on both sides.

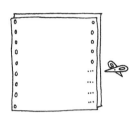

Take one strip from step 1 and thread it through the top hole in the front layer and then through the corresponding top hole in the back layer. Continue threading it through the holes down the side of the rectangles as if you were lacing a shoe.

At the bottom of the rectangle (skirt), tie the two ends in a bow.

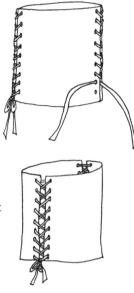

Repeat steps 4 and 5 on the opposite side.

Slip your skirt on and adjust the side laces as needed.

variations

attle things up a little and use pieces from two different T-shirts for the front and back panels of the skirt.

f you want to show more skin along the sides of your legs, cut the rectangles narrower before lacing them at the sides. (Don't worry. You won't get kicked out of Eden—though maybe out of school.)

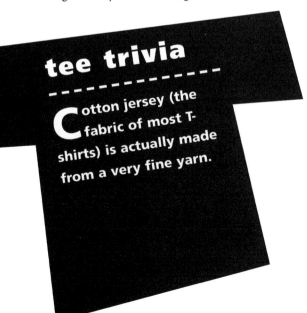

tee trivia

Cotton jersey (the fabric of most T-shirts) is actually made from a very fine yarn.

double-crosser

The bows at the hips of this skirt remind me of a string bikini bottom: girlie with a hint of danger. (One quick pull and . . .) Don't worry, I've got you covered. The side lacing will hold the skirt in place no matter how hard the tug. **LEVEL 3**

Turn the T-shirt inside out, lay it flat, and cut straight across the front just below the armholes through both layers. (You should have a wide tube of fabric.) Cut off the hemmed edge of the tube until the height is about 13".

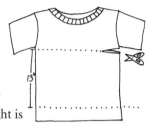

Divide your waist measurement by 2 (x). (Example: If your waist is 34", you'll be using a length of 17".) Center this length (x) across the top of the tube. Mark both sides (left and right) of the measurement with chalk, as shown.

Mark and cut (through both layers) a straight diagonal line from the bottom left corner of the tube to the left chalk mark. Repeat on the other side, marking and cutting diagonally from the bottom right corner to the right chalk mark (you now have two layers of trapezoid-shaped fabric).

Pin together the two layers along the angled edges. Sew using a whipstitch, leaving 6" open at the top of each side of the skirt.

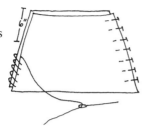

Slip the skirt on and tie a bow at each hip.

Turn the skirt right side out. About 1" in from the side edges, poke small holes 1" to 2" apart through both layers along the 6" openings.

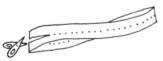

"A T-shirt is the epitome of young American style. A T-shirt in any guise . . . is young."

—designer Marc Jacobs

From the rest of the T-shirt (or, even better, if you have scraps left over, from a different-colored shirt) cut two strips, 1" to 1½" wide and at least 24" long.

variations

Starting at the bottom of one 6" opening, lace one of the strips up the side through the holes as if you were lacing a shoe. Repeat with the other strip on the opposite side.

nce you feel comfortable with measuring and cutting to your own dimensions, rather than cut the trapezoid parallel to the bottom of the T-shirt, cut it at an angle so that the text or design of the T-shirt is slightly off-kilter.

or a **no sew** version, use a more fitted shirt and cut across it at the bottom of the sleeves. Make 6" vertical openings at the top of each side of the shirt, poke holes, and lace up the sides as in step 7.

pocket rock it

This short skirt is casually versatile, loungy, or athletic. Take it to the beach; rock it at a show. The pocket gives you a chance to play around—a logo that looks too earnest emblazoned straight across your chest (like "St. Ann's Hospital Resident's Retreat, 2002") can look clever when you lay it at an angle across the front of your skirt. **LEVEL 3**

ingredients

- 2 T-shirts (1 S/M, 1 L/XL)
- measuring tape
- tailor's chalk
- scissors
- straight pins
- needle
- thread

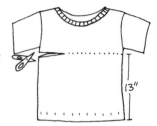

Turn the larger T-shirt inside out and lay it flat. Measure 13" up from the bottom hem and cut straight across the shirt (removing the top of the shirt and creating a rectangle).

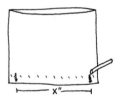

Divide your waist measurement by 2 (x). Center and mark that measurement across the bottom hem of the shirt. (This will become the top of your skirt.)

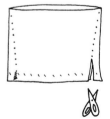

Mark and cut a straight line angled from one chalk mark to the upper corner on the same side of the rectangle. Repeat on the opposite side. (You should have two trapezoid-shaped layers of fabric.)

Pin and sew (using a whipstitch) the angled sides toegether, stopping just before the shirt's hem stitching.

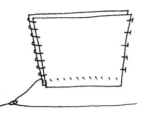

Using a running or zigzag stitch, sew along the top, bottom, and two sides of the pocket. Remove pins.

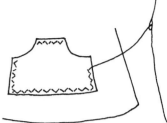

Turn the fabric right side out and flip the top and bottom. (You should have a short A-line skirt.)

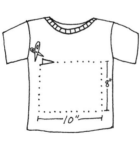

From the second T-shirt, cut two strips 1" wide and 24" long. Thread them through the front and back waistband of the skirt (the casings created by the hem of the first T-shirt). Tie on each side.

For the pocket, take the smaller T-shirt and cut a rectangle approximately 10" wide and 8" high through one layer.

variations

Fold the rectangle in half vertically. Mark and cut a 3" arc out of the corner, through both layers. Unfold it and center it right side out on the front of the skirt. Pin it in place.

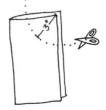

dd a pocket to the back of the skirt, too!

se the pocket pattern and attach it to other projects—T-shirts, tank tops, tubes . . . even a backpack.

next of pin

As we punk chicks get older, we face an inevitable identity crisis. Will we have to shop in the ladies' department and be sentenced to a lifetime of knee-length skirts? Next of Pin eases those growing pains: The shape of the skirt—straight and flared slightly above the knee—is mature without being dowdy. And the irreverent safety pins holding it together tell the world that you can be both punk rock and grown-up at the same time. **LEVEL 3**

Turn the T-shirt inside out and lay it flat. Cut off the sleeves just inside the seams and cut straight across the shirt just below the neck band. Cut a 1" strip off the bottom to use as a drawstring. Set aside.

Divide your waist measurement by 2 (x). Center that measurement at the top of the shirt and mark. Cut straight vertical lines up the sides of the shirt from the chalk mark to the bottom.

ingredients

- 1 T-shirt (L or XL)
- scissors
- measuring tape
- tailor's chalk
- straight pins
- needle
- thread
- 1 box safety pins (medium)

3 With right sides facing, pin the long side edges together.

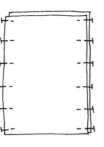

4 Measuring down the sides of the rectangle, make chalk marks about 13" and 17" from the top. Cut through both layers across the rectangle at those marks. You should have three double-layer smaller rectangles (still pinned at the sides).

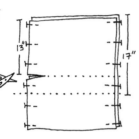

5 Sew along each of the six pinned edges using a whipstitch. Remove pins. You should have three tubes.

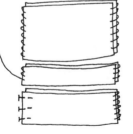

6 Turn each of the three tubes right side out. Use safety pins to reattach the tubes in the order they appeared as a T-shirt. Space the pins 1½" to 2" apart near the edge so that one tube hangs about ¾" below the other.

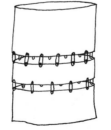

7 Add a row of safety pins around the top of the skirt—again, spaced 1½" to 2" apart. Thread the drawstring through the safety pins at the top, slip the skirt on, and tie the ends in a bow.

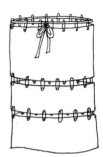

variations

t is possible to make this a **no sew** skirt, if the shirt you start with is small enough to fit comfortably around your hips without alterations. Follow the instructions without cutting or sewing the sides.

f you can't bear to grow up so soon (i.e., have a skirt go past your knees), just leave off the bottom strip.

ull the skirt up high for its transition into a **no sew** tube top. (*Note:* If you're short, this can even pass for a dress, provided it covers you in all the right places.)

lay with color and pin together tubes from three different T-shirts.

row, row, row your bows (gently down the seam)

After my sister and I finished making this skirt, we realized that it looked like the German flag (which has horizontal stripes of black, red, and gold). With the bows tied tight, this skirt will show off your *Knackpo,* German for "sexy bottom." Or combine blue, white, and red for the flag of Thailand (where sexy bottoms are called *gon su-ay*). Or green, yellow, and red for the flag of Bolivia, *qué culito.* So, celebrate your family's heritage (and their derrières) and start daydreaming about countries you'd like to wear—I mean, visit.

`LEVEL 4`

Lay two T-shirts flat and cut off the hemline of each. Cut three 5"-wide loops off the bottom of one shirt and two 5"-wide loops off the bottom of the second shirt.

ingredients

2 to 3 T-shirts
(L or XL, in different colors)
(*Note:* You'll need 3 to make any of the tricolored flags mentioned, but for easiest instructions, use 2 tees)

scissors

measuring tape

tailor's chalk

straight pins

needle

thread

Snip through one side of each loop to make five long strips. With chalk, center a length equal to your waist measurement (x) on each strip so that there is an equal amount of excess fabric on each side. (Example: If your waist measurement is 36" and the strips are 46" long, you will have 5" of fabric beyond the chalk markings on each side.)

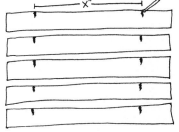

Lay out the strips, alternating colors and aligning the chalk marks.

Take the top two strips and lay them one on top of the other, right sides together. Pin along one edge between the chalk marks. Repeat using the third and fourth strips.

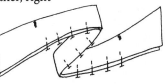

Pin the fifth strip to the fourth panel in the same manner

(right sides together, and between the chalk marks). Then pin the double row panel to the triple row panel. (Make sure the colors of your strips are still alternating.)

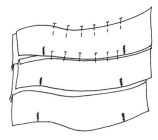

Sew the panels together ½" from the pinned edges using a running backstitch. Remove pins and flatten out the skirt.

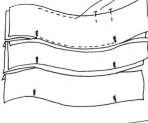

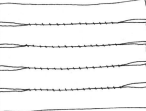

Wrap the skirt around your waist and tie the loose ends to their partners, all the way down. Rotate the skirt so the bows are slightly off-center.

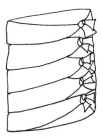

knot too shabby

Young lady, are you leaving the house in that? Because the holes expose skin, let me issue an official warning: This skirt may shift in flight. It's a good idea to have a friend on "booty duty," making sure nothing is revealed but the sides of your legs. Or, play it safe and wear a pair of leggings or funky stockings underneath. **LEVEL 2**

ingredients

1 T-shirt (XL)
scissors
measuring tape
tailor's chalk

1   Lay the T-shirt flat. Mark and cut (through both layers) two vertical lines from the top of the shirt to the bottom, just inside the sleeves.

2   Mark and cut a straight line across the shirt just below the neck band. Cut off the hem. Rotate the rectangles (both layers) so they're horizontal.

3   Divide your waist measurement by 2 and then subtract 2 (x). (Example: For a 32" waist, divide by 2 to get 16"; subtract 2 to get 14".)

Center that measurement along both long edges of the rectangle, mark it at both ends, and draw vertical chalk lines connecting the marks, as shown.

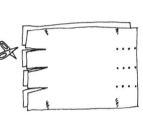

Along both sides of the skirt cut horizontal slits (through both layers) 4" apart, stopping at the chalk line.

Tie the loose ends to their partners, securing the back and front layers all the way down the sides.

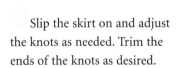

Slip the skirt on and adjust the knots as needed. Trim the ends of the knots as desired.

variation

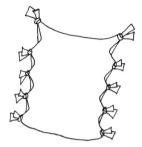

ead, shoulders, knees, and toes: conversion outfit alert! Wear it as a tank top by slipping it over your torso and tying the top two knots over your shoulders, as shown below.

skirt flirt

Breezy and flirtatious, this mini peasant skirt is charming, comfy, and a must-have for the beach. For the best effect, pick a T-shirt that has an appealing horizontal print or lettering across the chest (college name T-shirts are often ideal). Even though this project is rated 4, there's no need to be intimidated. Just be patient—it's actually easier than it looks. **LEVEL 4**

ingredients

- 1 T-shirt (L or XL)
- measuring tape
- scissors
- tailor's chalk
- needle
- thread
- straight pins
- 1 safety pin

Lay the T-shirt flat, cut off the hem, and cut a 10" to 12" tube off the bottom.

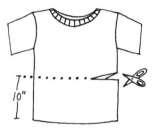

Using a ruler and chalk, measure and mark every 6" to 8" around the top edge of the tube. (*Note:* The important thing is to make an all the marks an equal distance apart so that the fabric gathers evenly around the circumference of the skirt.)

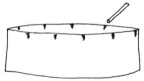

Baste around the circumference of the tube, ½" from the edge.

4 Measure your waist and divide by 2 (x). Gather the fabric by pulling the loose end of the thread while gently pushing the fabric in the opposite direction. The gathered width should equal x. Try to keep the gathers even and unbunched. Turn inside out and set aside.

7 Measure and mark the same number of segments you made in step 2 around the bottom edge of the second tube. Make sure the marks are an equal distance apart.

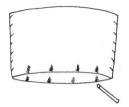

5 Turn the remaining part of the T-shirt inside out and measure and mark a rectangle whose width is equal to x (above) and whose height extends to just below the neck band. Cut along the markings through both layers.

8 With right sides together, place the smaller tube inside the larger tube, aligning the chalk marks.

9 Pin and sew the tubes together using a running backstitch, going over the basting stitch to secure the gathers. Remove pins.

6 Pin the short edges of the rectangle together, right sides facing, and try on to check for fit. Then sew along the pinned edges using a running backstitch or a whipstitch. Remove pins and turn right side out.

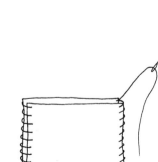

continued

Unfold the skirt, keeping it inside out. Fold the top edge down about 1" to make a waistband and sew in place, using a whipstitch. Turn the skirt right side out.

Make two small snips (through only the top layer of fabric) 2" apart at the center front of the skirt waistband.

Use the hem you cut in step 1 as the drawstring. Thread it through the waistband casing.

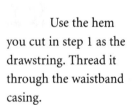

Slip the skirt on and tie it in front.

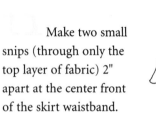

variations

se two different T-shirts and make tiers of different colors or patterns.

ind an XL T-shirt, cut 12" off the bottom, make gathers along the bottom of the existing skirt, and, following steps 8 to 10, add a third tier for more length. And yes, you can keep adding till you hit the floor.

ake a longer A-line skirt and add a small (3") ruffle. Add a flower blossom or bud as further embellishment (see projects 89 and 90).

triple-layer cake

This tiered skirt, as sumptuous as a triple-layer cake, taunted me all last spring. It was in every boutique window, with tempting silk chiffon layers in frosting colors— pinks, creams, and mint greens. Finally, I'd had enough. I went home and created my own "recipe" using the ingredients I had on hand (T-shirts, what else?). Well-worn jersey can be as soft as silk, and it doesn't need to be dry-cleaned. Have your cake and eat it, too: This skirt doubles as a tube top. Yum. **LEVEL 4.5**

Lay one T-shirt flat, cut off the hem, then cut 12" off the bottom, creating a tube.

Cut open the tube along one side to make a wide rectangle and cut the rectangle to the same width as your waist measurement (x).

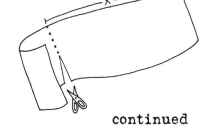

continued

----
ingredients
----
2 T-shirts (L or XL)

measuring tape

tailor's chalk

scissors

straight pins

needle

thread

Fold the rectangle in half, short edge to short edge, and right sides facing. Pin and sew the edges together using a whipstitch.

Using a ruler and chalk, measure and mark every 6" to 8" around the top edge of each tube. (*Note:* The marks should be an equal distance apart.)

Remove the pins, turn the tube right side out, and set it aside. (This is the inner tube to which the three tiers will be attached.)

Baste along one edge of each tube ½" from the edge.

From the first T-shirt, cut off a 7"-wide strip from the bottom, through both layers. On the second shirt, cut off the hem, then cut two 7"-wide strips off the bottom.

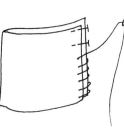

Gather the fabric by pulling the loose end of the thread while gently pushing the fabric in the opposite direction. Try to keep the gathers even and unbunched. The gathered circumference should be about x. Set the three gathered tubes aside.

On both edges of the inner tube (step 4), mark as you did in step 6. Then draw a line connecting the top and bottom edge markings.

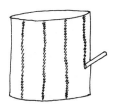

Insert the inner tube through one of the gathered tubes, with both right sides out. Align the chalk marks on both tubes. Pin the gathered tube on top of the inner tube so the edges overlap 1", as shown.

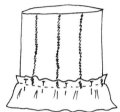

Fold the top edge down 1" over the gather to hide it, then sew it down using a whipstitch.

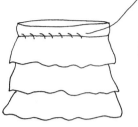

Repeat step 10 with second gathered tube, positioning it 6" from the bottom of the inner tube.

Slip your skirt on and give it a whirl.

Repeat step 10 again with the last gathered tube, postioning it 1" below the waistline, or top edge, of the inner tube.

variations

Check that the tiers are evenly spaced and sew along the pinned edges with a zigzag stitch or whipstitch, securing the gathered outer ruffles to the inner tube. (*Note:* Use small stitches to keep the gathers in place.) Remove pins and basting stitches.

ake a longer skirt and add more layered ruffles. You can even make an ankle-length skirt for crazy ruffle-mania. (Sew multiple tubes together for the inner structure.) Just be sure to let the skirt get a little wider toward the bottom so you can still walk around in it.

ull the skirt up around your torso for a tube top. If you need to secure it, run a drawstring through the folded-over "waist-band" you made in step 14.

petal pusher

If your closet were a garden, your work clothes would be the vegetables and this skirt would be your prize tulip. It's all about cultivating the accents. Try alternating solid-color "petals" with patterned ones—I matched a pink tee with a green tee to bring out the corresponding colors in my Ben & Jerry's T-shirt. Wear a low-slung studded belt with Petal Pusher to add some edge to the flowery femme look.

LEVEL 5

Lay a medium (or size small if you're especially petite) T-shirt flat and cut 13" off the bottom so that you have a tube. (This will eventually be the waistband.)

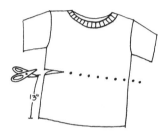

---
ingredients
---

3 T-shirts (1 S or M for waistband, 2 L for petals)

ruler

tailor's chalk

scissors

straight pins

needle

thread

2 To make the petals, cut five rectangles each 12" wide and 10" high out of the three T-shirts (the two remaining uncut shirts plus the scraps from the first).

3 Stack the five rectangles (petals) right sides up and round off two of the corners, as shown.

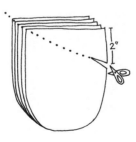

4 Mark and then cut a diagonal line from one of the remaining corners to 2" below the other remaining corner, as shown. (*Note:* If you prefer cutting the petals separately, draw and cut a petal shape out of an old newspaper page and use it as a pattern.)

5 Place the straight edge of each petal (right side down) against the cut edge of the tube (right sides together) and pin. The petals should overlap the tube edge about ½" and overlap each other about 3" on either side. (*Note:* If you find that five petals aren't enough to go all the way around the skirt, add a sixth or seventh petal.)

6 Sew the pinned edges together all the way around the skirt using a running backstitch. Remove pins.

7 Slip the skirt around your hips and fold the waistband down to cover up the petal seams.

variations

u se more T-shirts and make each petal a different color.

f or a different (not rounded) sort of flap, leave the corners of the rectangle squared before you complete step 4.

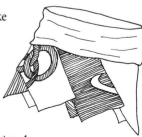

flare thee well

abric, fabric, fabric. Here's a case where more *is* more—you want to use several T-shirts, so this swank circle skirt has as much flounce and flair as possible. Think twirling till you're dizzy. The wide fold-over yoke arranged just so gives you license to strut down the street with the utmost hipster pride, but beware: This skirt may compel you to suddenly spin around in the middle of the sidewalk, destroying any illusion of cool. **LEVEL 5**

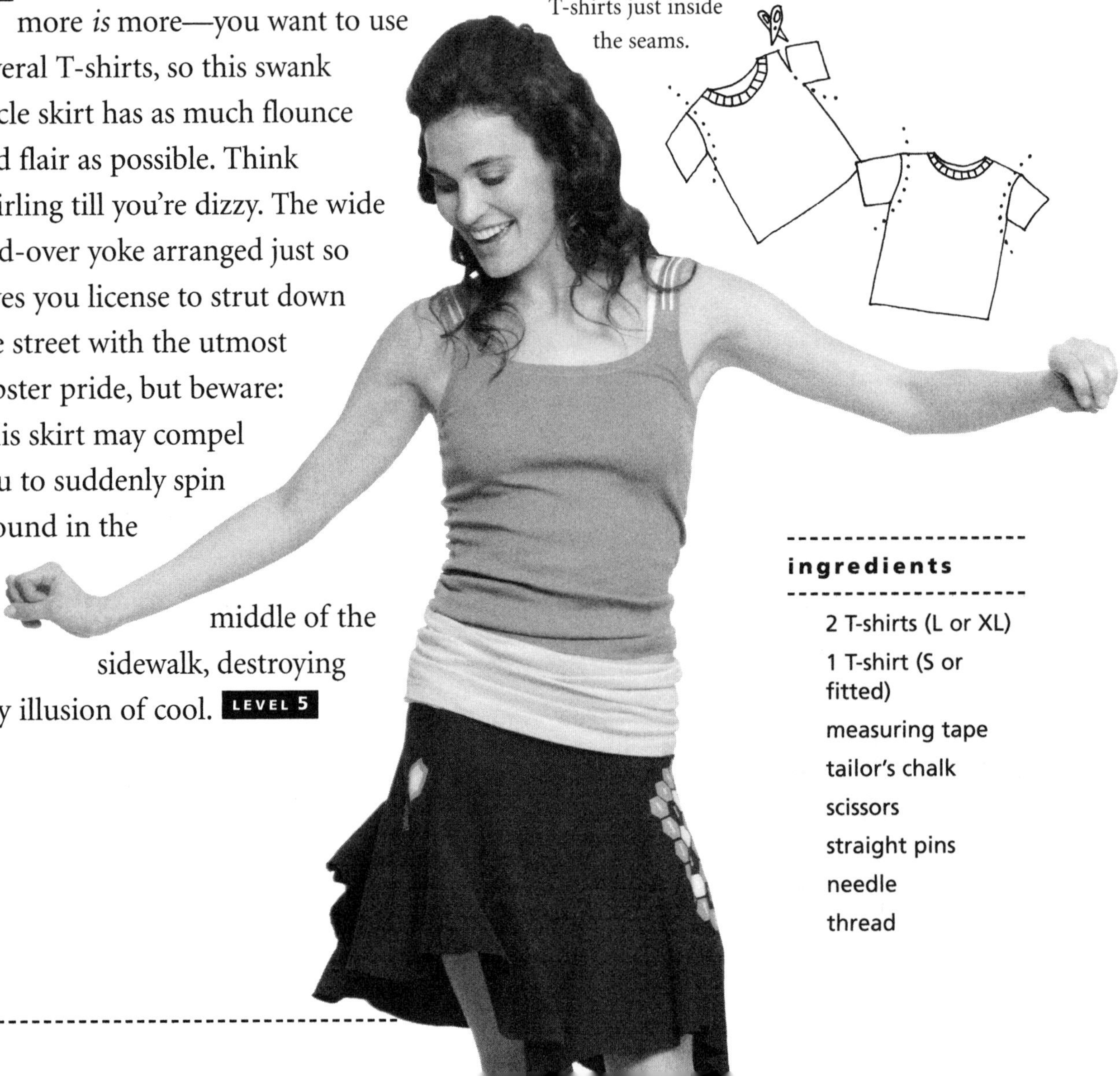

Cut the sleeves off the two larger T-shirts just inside the seams.

ingredients

2 T-shirts (L or XL)

1 T-shirt (S or fitted)

measuring tape

tailor's chalk

scissors

straight pins

needle

thread

Lay the sleeveless shirts flat on top of each other. Mark and cut (through all four layers of fabric) a 20" square.

variations

or a beach-bound tube top sundress, pull the waistband up your torso, snip two small holes in what was the bottom hem of the third T-shirt, and run a drawstring through it. Or, if you want more security, add straps.

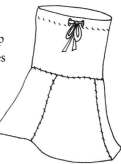

Mark and round off one of the corners by cutting (through all four layers) a wide arc between the two adjacent corners, as shown.

or extra flounce, add another arcing "wedge" or two. Just be sure to shorten the top width of the other wedges so the waist size isn't increased.

celebri-tee corner

From time to time, a T-shirt can really hit it big. In 2004 the tee slogan "My Boyfriend Is Out of Town" was in with the in-crowd, gracing the chests of such fashion-forward stars as **Drew Barrymore**, Mary-Kate Olsen, Famke Janssen, Britney Spears, and Kelly Osbourne (to name a few).

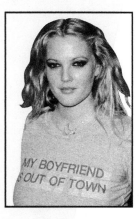

Divide your waist measurement by 6 (x). (Example: For a 30" waist, divide by 6 to get 5".) Mark that measurement along each edge of the uncut corner (the one across from the rounded corner).

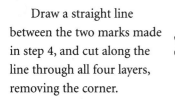

Draw a straight line between the two marks made in step 4, and cut along the line through all four layers, removing the corner.

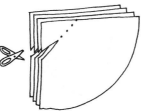

continued

6 Separate the four wedges and arrange them (right side down) in a large circle as shown, alternating the panels of the two shirts.

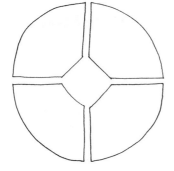

7 Pin two of the wedges together along their straight edges (right sides together). Continue until all four edges are pinned, creating a ring of fabric.

8 Sew the four pinned edges together using a whipstitch. Remove pins and turn right side out.

9 Lay the smaller T-shirt flat and cut 14" off the bottom, creating a tube large enough to fit over your hips.

10 Place the ring of fabric (the skirt) inside the tube with the right side of the skirt facing the wrong side of the tube. Pinch the raw edges of the skirt and tube together and pin in place.

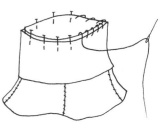

11 Sew the edges together using a zigzag stitch or whipstitch. Remove pins.

12 Slip the skirt over your hips, fold the waistband down on itself, and give it a twirl.

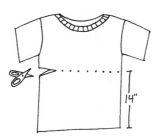

mud flap

If you've never lived through New England mud season, you may not understand the full significance of those rubber flaps hanging behind tires. Mud splatters everywhere—on cars, road signs, and, if you're the puddle-jumping type, even on skirts. But mud season signals the coming of spring and a change in wardrobe. That's right, skirts are now in session. This simple, sexy asymmetrical skirt is a great excuse to bring those winter legs out of hibernation. Kick up your heels and get some dirt on that skirt. **LEVEL 2**

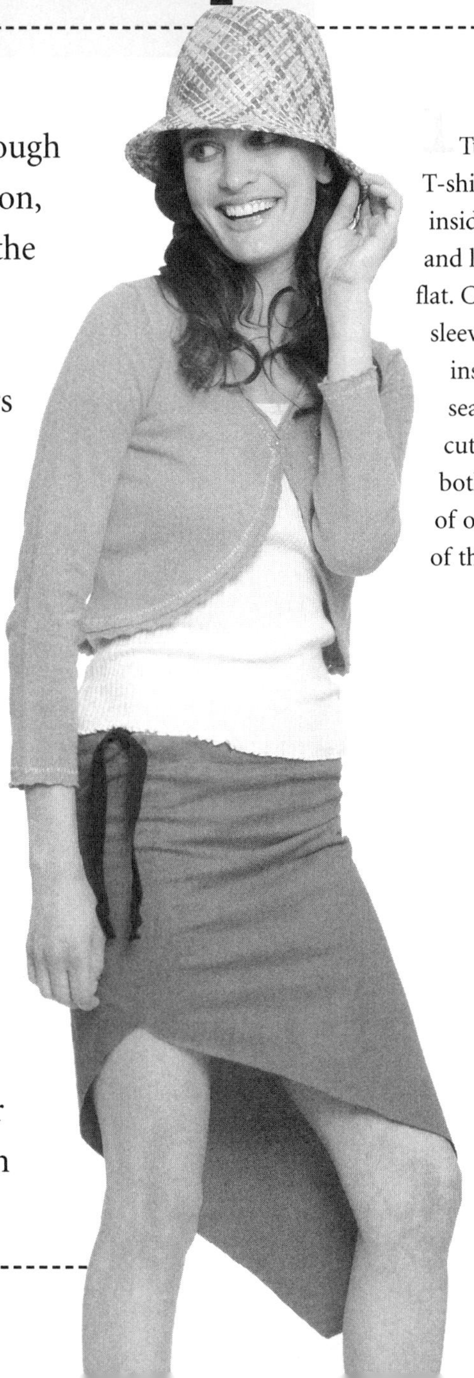

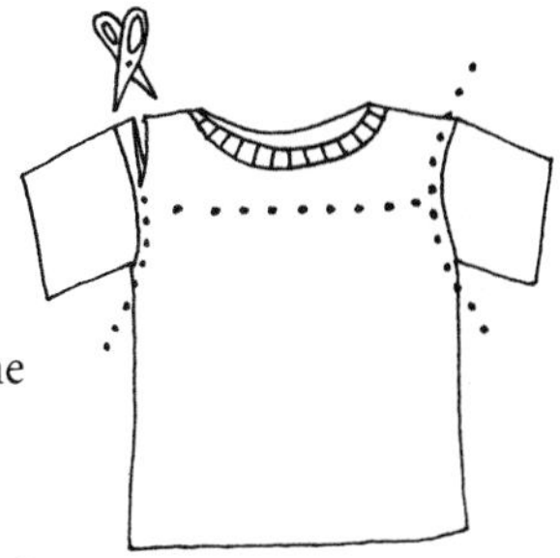

Turn the T-shirt inside out and lay it flat. Cut off the sleeves just inside the seams and then cut straight across, through both layers, from the middle of one armhole to the middle of the other.

continued

ingredients

1 T-shirt (L or XL)
scissors
measuring tape
tailor's chalk
needle
thread
straight pins
safety pin

Divide your waist measurement by 2 (x). (Example: For a 32" waist, divide by 2 to get 16".) Mark the measurement (x) along the bottom edge, as shown. Draw a vertical line from the chalk mark to the top of the fabric. Then cut along the line through both layers.

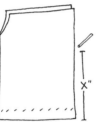

Starting from the bottom, measure about 14" (or the length from your waist to mid-thigh), mark with chalk, and pin.

Sew up the side edge from the hem of the shirt to the chalk mark made in step 3 using a whipstitch. (*Note:* Do not sew through the hem.)

Turn the shirt right side out and lay it flat with the hem of the shirt at the top. Rotate so the seam from step 4 is slightly toward the center.

Measure 10" from the top of the skirt down along the folded edge closest to the seam and mark with chalk.

tees in the movies

A Streetcar Named Desire (1951): "Stella!" may be one of the most frequently quoted movie lines, and Marlon Brando's sweaty T-shirt is one of the most frequently emulated looks.

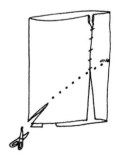

Draw a diagonal line with chalk and ruler from the 10" chalk mark to the bottom of the other folded side of the skirt. Cut through both layers along that line.

Re-rotate the skirt so the seam is back on the side. (The shortest point of the skirt will be slightly toward the front.)

variations

or a **no sew** (and shorter) version, use a T-shirt that fits perfectly around your hips.

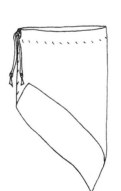

Cut a drawstring strip approximately 48" long from the remaining fabric, and thread it through the original T-shirt hem.

elebrate V-Day by cutting a symmetrical "V" shape out of the bottom of the skirt (through both front and back layers) so that the fabric comes to a point right between your knees.

Now slip the skirt on, tie the drawstring, and wear.

dd an asymmetrical flare by cutting a right isosceles triangle from another T-shirt. (The measurement of the base of your triangle should be equal to the length of the Mud Flap angle.) Sew the edges together and let the fabric fall where it may (the triangle wedge of fabric should ruffle a bit), and dance the night away!

diamonds in the rough

Learning to make your own clothes is a little like learning geometry (but with more of a payoff). You have to think about squares, rectangles, circles . . . and, in this project, diamonds. Diamond inserts make the bottom of this knee-length skirt flare out (always flattering to the hips and thighs), culminating in a charming witches-on-broomsticks effect.

LEVEL 5

Turn one of the T-shirts inside out (the one you want to be the main body of the skirt), and lay it flat. Mark and cut straight lines up the sides of the shirt just inside the sleeve seams from the top to the hem.

Measure 24" from the bottom of the shirt, then cut across the shirt through both layers.

ingredients

- 2 T-shirts (L)
- scissors
- ruler
- tailor's chalk
- straight pins
- needle
- thread
- 1 safety pin

Rotate so the hem is at the top (it will be the waistband). Starting just below the hem, pin, with right sides in, 13" down the sides. (The remaining unpinned edges should be about 11" long.)

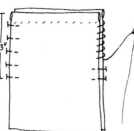

Sew the pinned edges together using a whipstitch, leaving 1" open at the top (the hem). Remove pins.

Mark and cut two 11"-long slits from the bottom of the skirt, spaced an equal distance apart evenly across the front. Do the same across the back. (You now have six slits around the base of the skirt.)

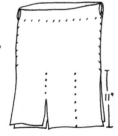

Cut the bottom hem off the second T-shirt (to be used as a drawstring). Across the front of the shirt, measure and draw three diamond shapes, each 15½" tall and 5½" wide at the widest point (crossing at 4", as shown). The two long sides of each

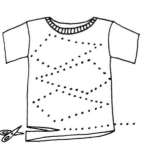

diamond should measure about 11" long. (*Note:* If it's easier, cut a pattern from a piece of newspaper and pin it on the fabric.) Remember: Sketch the diamonds on the shirt before cutting so that you make sure all three fit.

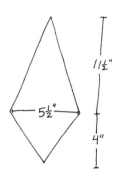

Cut through both layers so you have six diamonds. Into each slit cut on the skirt in step 5, pin the point of the longer side of one diamond at the very top of the slit, overlapping the edges ½". Both pieces should have the wrong sides facing up. Continue pinning each side of the slit to a side of the diamond, overlapping the edges ½". (The widest part of the diamond should meet the bottom edge of the skirt.) Repeat for each slit. Sew the pinned edges together using a running backstitch. Remove the pins.

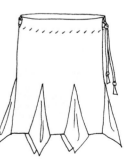

Turn the skirt right side out and, starting at one side opening, thread the drawstring through the original hem of the T-shirt. Slip the skirt on and tie at the side.

This skirt is a trip. It's better than a scrapbook—it's a wearable monument to your adventures. Gather up all the T-shirts from the places you've been— the Grand Canyon with the family, Mardi Gras in New Orleans, gambling (or a quick walk down the aisle) in Vegas, the Venice Beach boardwalk, that random café in Saratoga . . . This skirt is so lightweight and comfy, you can wear it on your next road trip. (And it packs well, too!) **LEVEL 4**

tee trivia

A T-shirt bearing the I ♥ NY logo (designed by Milton Glaser in 1976 to promote the image of the city) was presented to Fidel Castro when he visited the U.N. in 1979.

ingredients

- 6 T-shirts (L or XL, with travel theme graphics)
- measuring tape
- tailor's chalk
- scissors
- straight pins
- needle
- thread

1 Divide your waist measurement by 6 and then add 1 (x). (Example: For a 30" waist, divide by 6 to get 5"; add 1 to get 6".) Lay the T-shirts flat and cut a 24"-long (slightly trapezoidal) strip from each one, using the measurement x for the width of the top of each strip. The width of the bottom of each strip should be 1½" wider than the top. *Note:* Use a paper pattern if you prefer.

2 Arrange the strips next to each other in the order you'd like them to appear on the skirt and pin them together along the long edges (right sides together).

3 Sew along the pinned edges ½" from the edges using a running backstitch. Remove the pins and turn the skirt right side out.

Measure 4½" up from the bottom of one of the shirt remnants and cut a strip through both layers, as shown. Trim the strip until it is 1" longer than your waist measurement.

5 Sew the ends of the strip together (right sides in) ½" from the edge, using a running backstitch.

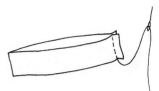

6 Fold the top edge of the tube down to meet the bottom, wrong sides together. You should have a double-layer tube about 2¼" wide.

7 Place the tube around the outside top of the skirt, lining up the unfinished edges with the top edge of the skirt. Pin in place.

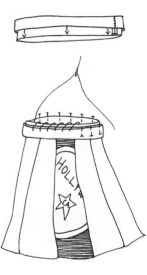

8 Sew along the pinned edges, close to the edge using a zigzag stitch or whipstitch. Remove the pins.

9 Pull on the skirt and head for the open road!

material girl

Some girls try and some girls lie, but I don't let them play. Only girls who save old T-shirts make my rainy day. Here's a simple rainy-day project with a funky extended seam that flaps around when you start dancing to Madonna's *The Immaculate Collection.* (Imagine that, a tight skirt where the *excess* material becomes the compelling detail.) **LEVEL 2.5**

ingredients

1 T-shirt (L or XL)
scissors
measuring tape
straight pins
tailor's chalk
needle
thread

Lay the T-shirt flat. Cut through both layers on a horizontal line, from the bottom of one sleeve to the bottom of the other. Cut off the hem just above the stitching and then cut through one side of the tube to make a rectangle.

Along the top of the rectangle (the top of the skirt), center and mark (with straight pins) your waist measurement (x).

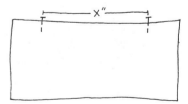

3 Fold the rectangle in half horizontally (wrong sides in) so that the two pins you placed in step 2 match up. Draw a straight line down from the pins, perpendicular to the top and bottom of the skirt. Pin the two layers together along the line.

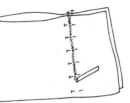

4 Sew along the pinned line using a running backstitch. Remove pins. (You should have a wide external seam.)

5 Slip the skirt on, trim the flaps if you like, and give it a twirl!

tee trivia

Do, re, mi fa, so, la, TEE! Dozens of songs, raps, and other odes have been written about the T-shirt. From the aptly titled "T-shirt," (Destiny's Child) to Adina Howard's sexy "T-shirt and Panties," to ZZ Top's "Girl in a T-shirt" and Frank Zappa's "Fembot in a Wet T-shirt," the tee crosses musical genres, representing themes of lost love, life on the streets, hot girls, and backyard barbecues . . . even T-shirt tan lines.

variations

experiment with the size T-shirt that you start with. The wider the shirt, the more Material Girl you can get—more fabric equals a flappier skirt.

angle the seam out from the waistband slightly so that the skirt isn't as clingy.

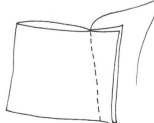

for a **no sew** version, use safety pins down the length of the skirt.

alphabet city

Where Sesame Street
intersects Avenue B:
A for A-line skirt
B for Bold statement
C for Creativity
D for Downtown . . .
*(Now I know my ABCs,
next time won't you
sing with me?)*

---

ingredients

---

1 T-shirt (L or XL)

2+ T-shirts with text

scissors

measuring tape

tailor's chalk

straight pins

needle

thread

Turn the T-shirt inside out and lay it flat. Cut off the sleeves just inside the seams and then cut straight across, through both layers of fabric, right below the armholes.

Add 1" to your waist measurement and then divide by 2 (x). Center the calculated length along the top edge of the rectangular tube you made in step 1. Mark both ends of the measurement with chalk.

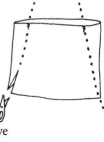

Make a diagonal cut through both layers, starting from the bottom left corner of the rectangle to the left chalk mark. Repeat on the right side of the rectangle. (You now have two layers of trapezoid-shaped fabric.)

With right sides together, pin and sew up both sides of the trapezoid with a whipstitch. Remove the pins and turn the skirt right side out.

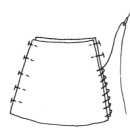

From the other T-shirts, cut out printed letters of the alphabet. Arrange and pin them in order around the base of the skirt about ½" above the bottom edge. (*Note:* Don't, under any circumstances, toss what's left of the T-shirts—save them for other projects.)

Sew the letters on the skirt with a running stitch or a whipstitch. (Or just tack them on four sides with a single stitch and knot.)

Remove any remaining pins, slip the skirt on, and go out and play—you've earned it.

variations

or a **no sew** version, make a miniskirt out of the bottom of a fitted tee (using the hem as a drawstring waist) and attach each letter with a safety pin or two.

eeling confident with your ABCs? Write a poem or quote Shakespeare around the base of the skirt instead. Or, add stripes instead of letters: Attach three strips from the same (or another) T-shirt, circumnavigating the skirt horizontally (or sewing them on a diagonal if you think you can't pull off horizontal stripes).

ake it straight to the top and appliqué a ransom note message across the front or back of a T-shirt.

bohemian wrapsody

The secret to bohemian chic is to make it seem like you don't care how you look but *somehow* always wind up looking gorgeous anyway. I call it ambivalently fashionable. "Oh, this?" you'll say offhandedly when someone admires the cool draping cut of this skirt. "I just wrapped part of an old T-shirt around me and pinned it with this button I got from my friend's band." And the best part is, it will be true. **LEVEL 1**

Lay the T-shirt flat and cut off the sleeves just inside the seams. Then, through the top layer only, cut straight across the front of the shirt just above the bottom of the armholes.

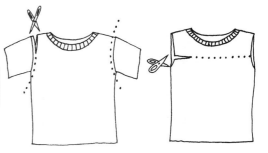

Cut straight across the back of the shirt just below the neck band. Separate the top of the shirt from the bottom, and toss the top aside.

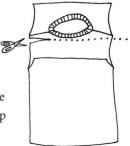

---

ingredients

---

1 T-shirt (L)

scissors

1 punk pin

1 safety pin

Cut through one side of the shirt from hem to bottom of armhole. Lay the piece flat and cut off the bottom hem just above the stitching.

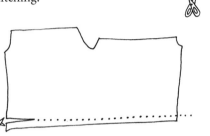

variation

se more safety pins (think kilt) or more punk pins (think funk).

With the straight edge at the bottom, wrap the fabric around your waist, overlapping it slightly in the front (the bottom of the remaining armhole should be at the back of the waist). Fold down any extra fabric at the top of the waistband. Use a punk pin to close the skirt at the waist, to the left or right of your belly button. (*Optional:* You may want to use an additional safety pin if you find that the wraparound is revealing a bit too much leg.)

Issey Miyake took no-sew to another level in 1999 with his A-Poc. The A-Poc (A Piece of Cloth) is a design concept that allows the customer to determine the exact fit of his or her T-shirt. Adjustments are made on a computer screen and transferred to a machine that produces the perfect customized shirt from a single piece of cloth without any cutting, sewing, or stitching.

I'm convinced the wrap skirt was invented by a woman, because only someone who understands firsthand our mood swings, weight fluctuation, and desire for clothes that are both practical and stylish could have come up with such an ingenius creation. The T-shirt wrap skirt is even more forgiving than most. Because it's adjustable *and* stretchy, it fits perfectly—no matter what. **LEVEL 4**

---

ingredients

- 3 T-shirts (L or XL)
- measuring tape
- tailor's chalk
- scissors
- straight pins
- needle
- thread

Add 15 to your waist measurement, and then divide by 3 (x). (Example: For a 36" waist, add 15 to get 51; divide by 3 to get 17".) Lay two of the T-shirts flat and cut out a rectangle (through both layers) from each with a length of 16" and a width corresponding to the measurement (x) above. Separate the four rectangles.

Place two rectangles (from different T-shirts) on top of each other, right sides together, and pin along one of the 16"-long edges. Sew along the pinned edge using a whipstitch. Remove pins.

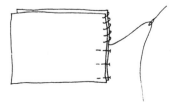

With right sides together, lay a third rectangle against one of the 16" edges of the pieces you just sewed and pin and sew as you did in step 2. Remove pins.

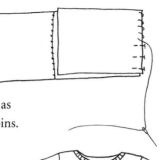

Lay the third T-shirt flat, cut off the hem just above the stitching, and cut an 8½" loop off the bottom. Cut through this loop, and then cut the strip in half lengthwise so you have two long strips, each 4¼" wide (for the two belt parts).

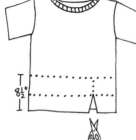

Fold the strips in half lengthwise, wrong sides out, and pin along the raw edges, leaving the ends open. Whipstitch the pinned edges.

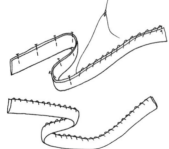

Turn the strips right side out and pin the end of one strip to the top outside corner of the third rectangle (sewn in step 3). It should be about 1" from the top edge and

should overlap the rectangle by 1½". Pin the second strip to the top corner of the adjacent rectangle, as shown.

Tack the strip ends to the skirt by using a running stitch to sew a 1¼" square through all layers, as shown.

One third of the way across the top edge of the skirt, make a 1¾"-high vertical slit ½" inch from the top.

Remove any remaining pins and wrap the skirt around your waist. Slip the end of one strip across the front of your waist, through the slit (from inside to outside), and around the back of your waist to the front, as shown.

Tie the two strips together at your side and trim the long one, if needed.

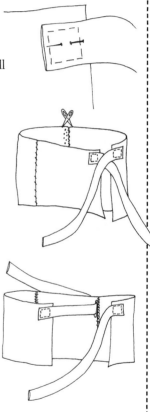

cinch city

Up the ante. Bright lights, all-night parties, high rollers calculating their odds at the craps table, the rain of coins at the winning slot machine, even the velvet Elvis. This skirt has that Vegas thrill with a high five to L.A. glamour, Chicago soul, and New York caché. Oh, forgive me, for I have cinched! **LEVEL 3.5**

Lay the T-shirt flat. Cut off the hem just above the stitching and then cut a 14" tube off the bottom.

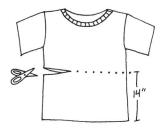

Cut through one side of the tube to make a long rectangle. Add 3" to your waist measurement, and mark that length along the long side of the rectangle, cutting off the excess.

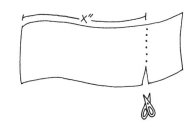

Censored: People have been kicked out of school and political conventions, even off airplane flights, for the T-shirts they've worn. In Miami, Florida, in 2004, a young man and his girlfriend were escorted from a flight when he refused to change or turn inside out a tee he was wearing that depicted *gasp!* a female breast!

---
ingredients
---

1 T-shirt
measuring tape
scissors
tailor's chalk
straight pins
needle
thread
1 safety pin

Fold the rectangle in half (right sides in, short edges together), pin along the edges, and sew a seam 1" to 1½" from the edge using a running backstitch.

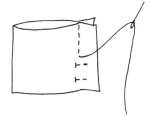

4 Open the seam flat and sew the 1" seam allowance to the skirt with a running stitch or whipstitch to create the drawstring casing.

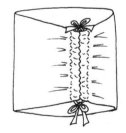

5 Cut two drawstrings from the rest of the T-shirt and thread one up each casing.

6 Turn the skirt right side out and try it on. Ruche the fabric as desired and tie both drawstring ends in bows.

variation

try using a contrasting color strip from your scrap pile or a ribbon as the drawstring.

your ass is grass

You may never make it to Hawaii. But even if you can't afford airfare to Maui, your thrift store T-shirt can get you twice the mileage. In the dead of winter, slip into this fringed thang, mix yourself a mai tai, put the hippest hula music on your playlist, and bask in a beach chair next to your radiator. Minus the tiki torches (fire hazard!) and the pig on the spit, you've got yourself a luau.

LEVEL 2

Turn the T-shirt inside out and lay it flat. Cut off the sleeves just inside the seams and the top of the shirt just below the neck band.

Divide your waist measurement by 2, center and mark that length (x) across the top of the shirt.

ingredients

1 T-shirt (L or XL)
scissors
measuring tape
tailor's chalk
needle
thread
masking or clear tape

3 Starting at one chalk mark, make a diagonal cut (through both layers) to the bottom corner of the shirt, as shown. Repeat on the opposite side to form an elongated trapezoid.

7 Carefully peel off the tape, try on your fringe skirt, and shake it up a bit.

4 Pin and sew (using a whipstitch) along the angled edges and turn the project right side out. You should have an A-line knee-length skirt.

variations

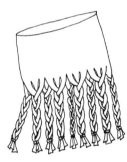

ut the number of fringe strips so they are divisible by three and braid them into tassles.

5 Measure approximately 10" up from the bottom of the skirt, and mark that length by attaching a piece of tape around the circumference of the skirt.

6 To make fringe, cut vertical strips about 1" wide, starting at the bottom and stopping at the piece of tape, all around the skirt.

or a **no sew** fringe-fabulous number, use a smaller T-shirt (the bottom of the shirt should fit snugly around your hips), cut off the top of the shirt just below the sleeves, turn it upside down, and cut some mini (2") fringe around the bottom.

tying up loose ends

This was another city street corner discovery: a girl, standing with her Polo-and-Docker-clad family of four, clearly on some sort of tourist mission, poring over a map of Lower Manhattan. And right in the middle of that khaki tundra, her carefully slashed and tied T-shirt skirt stood out like Gwen Stefani on safari. **LEVEL 4**

ingredients

- 1 T-shirt (L or XL)
- scissors
- measuring tape
- tailor's chalk
- straight pins
- needle
- thread

1 Turn the T-shirt inside out and lay it flat. Cut off the sleeves just inside the seams and then mark and cut (through both layers) a straight line from the middle of one armhole to the middle of the other.

2 Add 1" to your waist measurement and then divide by 2 (x) (Example: For a 35" waist, add 1 to get 36"; divide by 2 to get 18".) Center that measurement (x) along the bottom hem of the shirt. Mark both sides with chalk. (The bottom hem will become the skirt's waistline.)

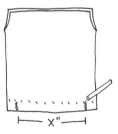

X"

Starting at one chalk mark, make a diagonal cut (through both layers) to the top corner, as shown. Repeat on the other side. (You should now have two layers of trapezoid-shaped fabric.)

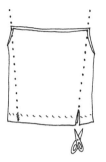

Pin the angled edges, right sides together, through both layers. Sew along the pinned edges using a whipstitch. Remove pins. Rotate the skirt so the hem becomes the waistband.

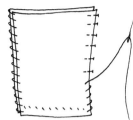

Mark a 6" line along each of the side seams, 4" from the bottom of the skirt. Then mark two more 6" lines equidistant from the sides of the skirt and from each other, also 4" from the bottom. Flip the skirt over and mark two lines, as you did on the front.

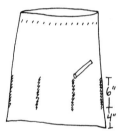

continued

tee trivia

Reuse, Reduce, Recycle: When environmentalism surfaced as a hot fashion issue in 2001, designer Giorgio Armani responded, making T-shirts out of organic cotton, hemp, and flax, complete with biodegradable buttons, labels, and stitching.

variation

For a shorter, more tube-shaped **no sew** version of the skirt, use the bottom tube of a smaller T-shirt as the skirt and make the slits only 3" or 4" high.

6 Next to each of the chalk lines, measure, mark, and cut parallel lines ½" to the right and left. Turn the skirt right side out.

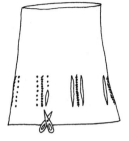

9 Repeat step 9 for the other five strips and bands. Tie matching strips in your hair (around a ponytail or two pigtails) as a finishing touch.

7 Cut six 15" by 1" strips from the T-shirt scraps. (For contrasting lacing, cut from other T-shirts or use ribbons.)

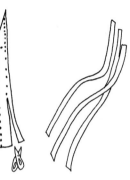

8 Take one strip and wrap it once around the top of one of the 1" bands created by cutting the slits in step 7—cross it in the front and wrap it around to the back, gently securing it at the top. Continue wrapping and crossing at the front and the back until you reach the bottom of the strip. Tie the ends in a small bow on the front.

the one-hour flapper dress

The "one-hour dress" (named for the time it took to make it) was designed in 1926 by the Women's Fashion Institute. Silhouettes in women's fashion had grown simpler in the 1920s—long, straight, and free-spirited. With advances in sewing technology, it became faster and easier for women to sew these refreshing new designs in their own homes. Did somebody say DIY?

flapper frenzy

There's no better way to spice up a sixth-grade U.S.-social-history-by-decade class project than with a homemade flapper costume. Here's the backstory: When my teacher was assigning decades, my best friend and I were hoping for the '60s or '70s, but we got stuck with the '20s—only to find that they were the cat's pajamas. Talk about liberation—women had just gotten the vote, they were baring their arms and legs like never before, and mass production of the Model T allowed them to take to the road. Who needed peace-loving hippies or disco dancers when we had short hemlines, short hair, and the Charleston, not to mention the most colorful slang in the joint? Playful, brazen, and jazzy—this dress is the bee's knees. **LEVEL 5**

continued

---

ingredients

5 T-shirts (L or XL, all one color or mix it up)

measuring tape

tailor's chalk

scissors

straight pins

needle

thread

Choose two T-shirts to use for the main body of the dress, turn them inside out, and lay them flat. Cut 17" off the bottom of each. Cut off the hems.

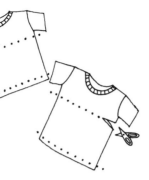

Make a vertical cut up one side of each tube, creating two matching, equal size rectangles. Add 1" to your chest measurement (x) and cut each rectangle to that length. Trim off the excess fabric.

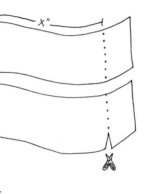

Fold both rectangles in half, wrong side out, short edges together. Pin and sew along the edges using a running backstitch ½" from the edge. Remove pins. You now have two matching tubes.

Turn one tube right side out and place it inside the other tube, which should still be wrong side out. Line up the seams and pin around the top edges. Sew along the pinned edges using a whipstitch.

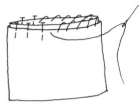

Remove pins and pull the outer tube up so that it's right side out and the inner tube is visible again. You now have an extra-long vertical tube. This will be the body of the dress.

Choose which half of the tube you'd like as the bottom part of your dress and mark 4" from its bottom edge around the circumference. Around the bottom of the dress, make vertical cuts from the edge to the 4" mark, spaced 1" apart. You now have the first layer of fringe. (The rest of the fringe will be added from this bottom layer up.)

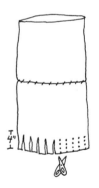

From three T-shirts, cut seven 5"-high tubes and snip through the sides so you have seven strips. Cut each strip to a length that equals your chest measurement and sew the sides as you did in step 3.

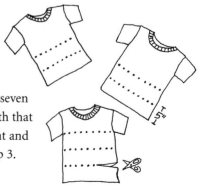

8 Mark each tube with chalk 4" from the bottom edge and cut fringe as you did on the bottom of the skirt in step 6.

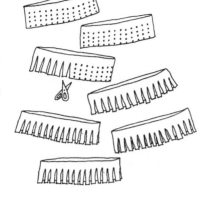

9 Pin one of the fringed tubes to the body of the dress so the bottom of its fringe aligns with the top of the slits from the preexisting fringe.

10 Sew along the pinned edge using a zigzag or running stitch. Remove pins.

11 Moving from the bottom to the top of the dress, repeat steps 9 and 10 with the remaining six tubes of fringe.

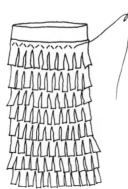

12 From the remaining T-shirt scraps, cut two strips 1" wide and at least 18" long. Pin the ends of the strips inside the front, top edge of the dress, about 4" to either side of the center. Sew using a boxed cross-stitch. Remove pins.

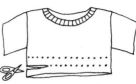

13 Try on the dress and adjust the straps so they are a good length for you. Pin the ends of the straps to the inside of the back, at the top edge (also about 8" apart.)

14 Carefully remove the dress and sew the straps in place on the back as in step 12. Remove pins.

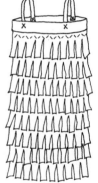

"American style is chic yet effortless. Nothing illustrates that better than the perfect T-shirt."

—designer Ralph Lauren

to a tee

You're never fully dressed without a *smile!* Presenting 16 projects that are the perfect accents for the body and the home. From leg warmers to hats, handbags to ponchos, checkbook covers to throw rugs.

Whether it's a jaunty handbag, a patchwork punk scarf, or a colorful throw pillow, the accent is a way of distinguishing yourself from the crowd—it's your punctuation mark. As today's clothing becomes more minimal and homogenized, it's the accessory that "makes the outfit," adding the right splash of color or personality. Likewise, as more and more people import living rooms straight from

Pottery Barn or IKEA, even a small handmade furnishing is a reminder that we adorn our rooms to express ourselves.

If eyes are the window to the soul, accessories are the window display. They exhibit the outlook and tastes of the person wearing them. I maintain that an accessory is not a frivolous extra, but an absolute essential. Whether it's an element of your outfit that changes from day to day (one day a belt, the next a bracelet) or a single accessory that becomes your signature look (that red leather watchband), people begin to associate you with your accent. Bono has his fly glasses, Salvador Dalí had his mustache, and Dorothy had those hot little ruby slippers. And who could forget *The Big Lebowski*'s rug—presoiled—that "really tied the room together"?

Many of the projects in this chapter don't wind up on your body at all, but dress your iPod or wood floor instead. With the structure dismantled, the T-shirt, reduced to a square (or circle, or strip) of cloth, becomes raw material. When you make accessories and home furnishings, you're giving old T-shirts a brand-new purpose, taking them from the sideshow back into the limelight.

And—I cannot stress this enough—the original T-shirt doesn't have to be that cool for your new creation to *look* cool. Cutting the words or the picture on a T-shirt out of context, deliberately leaving out some letters, reattaching the text upside down or at an angle, or juxtaposing different-color fabrics can turn the frumpy into the fabulously hip.

So if you don't have the time or inclination to go for the extreme closet or living room makeover, go for the accent—having a handmade accessory is the shortcut from completely generic to one-of-a-kind. The visual effect of an accessory speaks for you. And if you *make* that superhero wristband or throw pillow, the accessory speaks even louder. This chapter's a starter course.

go-go gauntlets

Even the name sounds hardcore. (Though they're called "arm warmers" in some circles, "gauntlets" is the preferred term among those who wear them.) They'll toughen up any night out from a Cinderella ball to a punk rock show, or turn the most mundane activity (typing a term paper or filing your taxes) into the bad-ass—adding just the right touch of superhero(ine) appeal. And it's not all fashion over function; gauntlets are practical, too—wear them in winter to cover that drafty area between your coat sleeve and mittens.

LEVEL 3

Mark and cut two rectangles at least 8" to 10" wide and 12" to 16" long from the sides of a T-shirt. (*Note:* The two pieces of fabric you cut off the sides of your Classic Punk tank, project 14, will work perfectly.)

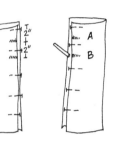

Fold the pieces in half lengthwise, right sides in, and pin along the edges. Mark with chalk at 2" (A) and 4" (B) along the open edges.

---

ingredients
---

1 T-shirt
ruler
tailor's chalk
scissors
straight pins
needle
thread

Using a whipstitch, sew the two pinned edges together. When you get to the first mark (A), sew along the edge of just one layer of fabric. At the second mark (B), resume sewing both layers together.

When you reach the end, reverse direction and restitch the seam. Again, at the second mark (B), sew only the single (unsewn) layer of fabric to finish off the thumbhole at A. Continue stitching through both pieces of fabric to the end. Repeat with other gauntlet.

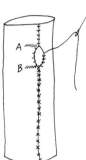

Knot the threads, snip off the ends, turn your gauntlets right side out, and slip 'em on for some immediate payoff.

variations

o show off your stitching, use a thread color that doesn't match the T-shirt fabric.

efore stitching the sides closed, appliqué a star or flower to the outer side.

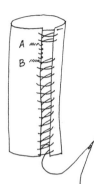

tee trivia

Celebrity spotting: In *Sex and the City* season six, episode one, Carrie Bradshaw claims she can't live without her T-shirt-material gauntlets.

knee huggers

They're back! No longer exclusive to the '80s or the ballerina set, leg warmers are charming legs from windy Chicago promenades to icy New York sidewalks. Now sunny California can get in on the action with knee huggers made out of T-shirts. Choose a solid-color tee or one with graphics, and, just like the leg warmer trend, your tee gets a second lease on life. **LEVEL 3**

ingredients

- 1 T-shirt (L)
- measuring tape
- tailor's chalk
- scissors
- straight pins
- needle
- thread

1 Measure your leg from just below your knee to the ground and add 1" (the length). Then measure around your leg just below the knee and add 1" (the width). Lay the T-shirt flat and measure and mark a rectangle with those dimensions. Cut through both layers to create two identical rectangles.

2 Fold one rectangle in half lengthwise, right sides together, and pin. Sew the sides together ½" from the edge, using a running stitch. (*Note:* If you prefer using the whipstitch, cut ½" off the edge you're about to sew, and go for it.)

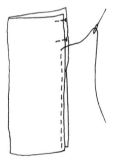

3 Fold the top of the leg warmer down about 1" and pin. Sew along the pinned edge using a small whipstitch.

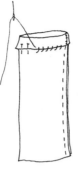

8 Try on the warmers, and tie the drawstrings to keep them from sliding down.

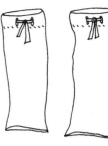

4 Repeat steps 2 and 3 with the other rectangle.

variations

5 From the rest of the T-shirt, cut two strips 1" wide and at least 10" longer than the width you measured in step 1.

1 engthen one leg warmer tube to about 26", trace and cut a circle of fabric 1" wider than the circumference of the bottom, and sew it (wrong sides out) to one end of the tube. Attach a strap and you've got a tote for your yoga mat.

6 Turn the leg warmers right side out and make two small incisions 1" apart (through one layer only) at the hemmed top of each one.

ake a shorter bag (no strap) for a wine or champagne gift cozy. Choose a T-shirt to suit the party—an Aloha tee for a luau or a city pride tee for the new neighbor.

7 Thread one drawstring through one hole, around the top of the leg warmer and out the second hole. Repeat.

the braided bunch

Here's the story of a lovely T-shirt that was cut into three lovely little strips. All of them were made of soft and well-worn fabric, a poly-cotton blend. Okay, before I take this any further: We're making a belt, not a family, and there will be no housekeeper named Alice. **LEVEL 1**

---
ingredients
---

1 T-shirt (L)
ruler
chalk
scissors
1 safety pin

Lay the T-shirt flat and cut three 1½"-to 2"-wide strips spiraling off the bottom. Each strip should be two rotations long (or about twice the size of your waist).

Knot the three long strips together at one end.

Use a safety pin to secure the knot to a pillow or the arm of a chair and braid the three strips together. To braid, alternate bringing the side strips over the center strip, moving the center strip to the side, as shown.

Leave about 6" at the end of your braid to tie into a knot. Remove the belt from the safety pin, wrap it around your waist, and tie the ends together. (*Note:* If the ends seem too long, trim one end of the belt and retie it.)

variations

nstead of using one T-shirt, use strips left over from other T-shirt projects for a more colorful palette.

implicity, simplicity, simplicity—take it one notch down. Use a single strip of T-shirt material, knot it at each end, and you've got a very classic string belt. Match it to a pair of gauntlets, hat, or bag for perfectly complementary accessories.

f you enjoy the braiding thing and want to take it to the next level, check out project 96, the Downward Spiral braided rug.

Beyond adding comfort and **style to your wardrobe, some T-shirts have mightier tasks. T-shirt fabrics can be knitted with yarn containing titanium dioxide, which filters harmful rays like a sunblock; others are infused with insecticides, scents, and moisturizers. Some T-shirts have working TV screens on the front. Some can even track a wearer's vital signs and produce real-time health results.**

punk poncho

"**I**s that a real poncho ... I mean, is that a Mexican poncho or a Sears poncho?" Our answer to Frank Zappa's sardonic query: Neither. Nor will it bear any resemblance to the paper bag poncho you made in second grade. A poncho is one of those great one-size-fits-all garments. Curl up in it as if it were a security blanket, soar around like a superhero, or pop in the mariachi music, mix up a mojito, and throw yourself a Cinco de Mayo party!

LEVEL 3

Turn one of the T-shirts inside out, lay it flat, and mark and cut (through both layers) an 18" by 24" rectangle (making two identical rectangles).

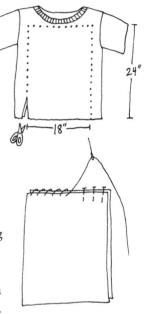

Pin the two rectangles together along the top (18") edge, and sew, using a whipstitch. Remove the pins, but keep the fabric folded so that it still looks like one 18" by 24" rectangle.

---
ingredients
---

2 T-shirts (L)
ruler
tailor's chalk
scissors
straight pins
needle
thread

3 Lay the second T-shirt flat. Mark and cut (through only one layer of fabric) a single 18" by 12" rectangle.

4 Fold this rectangle in half lengthwise (right sides together), creating an 18" by 6" folded rectangle.

5 Pin one 18" side to the bottom of one of the 24" sides of the larger rectangles, as shown.

6 Flip the rectangles over to pin the other 18" side to the bottom of the other 24" side.

(back)

7 Sew the pinned edges together with a whipstitch. Remove the pins and turn the garment right side out. (Ta-da! It's a poncho.)

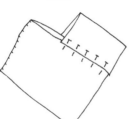

8 Along the bottom of the poncho about ½" in from the edge, poke or snip holes with the points of your scissors about 1½" apart.

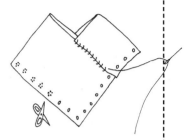

9 For the fringe, cut between 58 and 64 small strips (1" wide by 5½" long) from the remainders of the two T-shirts.

10 Take one strip, fold it in half, and force the looped end about halfway through one of the holes (from the outside to the inside). Thread the two ends around the edge of the poncho and through the loop, as shown. Pull them gently so the fringe is secured.

11 Continue around the perimeter of the poncho until you've had your fill of fringe.

Optional: For the more traditional fringe, make 2"- to 3"-long vertical cuts into the edge, about 1" apart.

scarf it up

T-shirts are generally associated with the warmer months of spring and summer. Here's your chance to expand the definition of "T-shirt weather" by bracing yourself against those blistering wintry days (or mildly chilly autumn ones) with a T-shirt scarf. This 64" scarf is also small-scale practice for the Patchwork Punk blanket, project 88. **LEVEL 3**

1 Lay both T-shirts flat, and measure and mark with chalk a 16" by 16" square on the front of each. Then divide each square into four 8" by 8" squares.

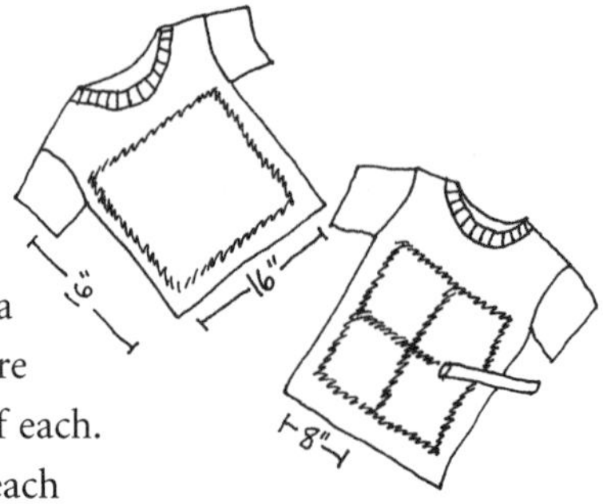

16"
6"
8"

2 Cut along the chalk lines, through both layers. You'll end up with eight squares (front and back layers) from each T-shirt.

ingredients

- 2 T-shirts (L, in different colors or patterns)
- tailor's chalk
- ruler
- scissors
- needle
- thread

3 Place two different-color squares right sides together and sew along one edge using a whipstitch. (You now have one 8" by 16" rectangle.) Repeat until you have eight 8" by 16" rectangles.

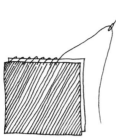

4 With right sides together, sew two rectangles along one 8" edge so that the colors of the squares continue to alternate. Repeat until you have four longer rectangles (about 8" by 32").

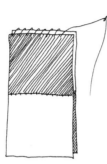

5 With right sides together, sew two of the 8" by 32" strips together along one 8" edge. Repeat with the other two strips. (You should now have two patchwork strips that measure approximately 8" by 64".)

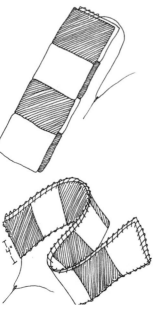

6 Place the two strips on top of each other (right sides together) and sew together with a whipstitch around all four edges, leaving 4" open (unsewn).

Pull the scarf through the 4" opening to turn it right side out and stitch the 4" open edges closed with a small whipstitch.

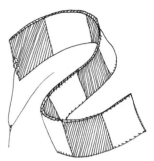

It's a wrap! Try it on.

variations

dd tassels for a fancy fringe effect. Cut twelve strips of fabric 12" by 1". About ½" from the edge, along the scarf ends, snip holes 1" apart. Fold the strips in half and poke the looped ends through each of the holes. Without pulling the loop all the way through, thread the two ends around the edge of the scarf and through the loop. Pull ends tight. (See Punk Poncho, project 76.)

or a simpler (thinner) scarf, make only one strip to wrap around your neck. (Add some no-fuss fringe to the ends by simply making 2"-long parallel cuts 1" apart.)

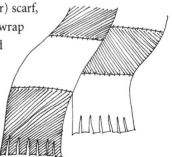

fit to be tied

This hat is a cinch, in both senses of the word. All you need are scissors and a T-shirt. And since you'll be using only a sleeve of the T-shirt, you'll have plenty of material left over to make a skirt to match. Or, use the other sleeve for a matching hat. Or a small change purse. Or . . . oh, the possibilities are endless.

Note: Try the sleeve on your head—with T-shirt still attached—to make sure it's the right size before you commit to the project.

LEVEL 1

Cut off one sleeve of the T-shirt just inside the seam. Cut off the hem of the shirt, then cut a 24" strip for a drawstring. Set the rest of the shirt aside for another project.

---
ingredients
---

1 T-shirt
(L or XL)
scissors

"Be daring, be different . . . assert imaginative vision against the play-it-safers, the creatures of the commonplace, the slaves of the ordinary."

—Cecil Beaton, fashion designer and photographer

Around the entire *interior* hem of the sleeve, make small (¼") incisions (through only one layer) about 1" apart .

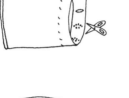

As if you were tightening a drawstring bag, pull both ends so the holes pucker closed ("just cinch it") and tie the ends in a bow.

Thread the drawstring in and out of the small holes around the hem.

Try on your hat, rolling the unfinished hem to hide it. Leave the drawstring ends long or trim them short.

tee trivia

A rose by any other name . . . Gracing its cover in 1963, the T-shirt was nicknamed the "summer sweater" by *Elle* magazine.

variations

find a colorful ribbon to use as the drawstring.

use the sleeve of a small or medium T-shirt, and follow the same steps to make a great baby gift. (Or, if your head doesn't have the dimensions that my family is blessed with, maybe this is the hat for you.)

check this

Writing checks usually happens in bulk, around that time of the month when you're paying the phone, gas, electricity, Internet, cable, rent, or mortgage bills. Ugh. Make the experience a little more comfy-cozy with a checkbook case made out of the comfiest-coziest T-shirt material. It won't wash away the money-spending blues, but it'll help. **LEVEL 3**

ingredients

- 1 T-shirt
- ruler
- tailor's chalk
- scissors
- straight pins
- needle
- thread

Mark and cut an 8½" by 10¼" rectangle through only one layer of the T-shirt. Set the rest of the shirt aside for another project.

Lay the rectangle flat, wrong side up, fold over 1" along the 10¼" sides, and pin in place. (You now have a 6½" by 10¼" rectangle.)

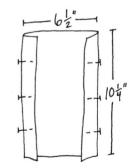

Flip the rectangle over and fold over 1¾" along each of the 6½" edges toward the center. Pin the four folded over pieces. Remove the pins you placed in step 2.

variations

ry appliquéing some shapes onto the outside panel of the checkbook cover.

Sew along the pinned edges using a small whipstitch. Remove pins and turn right side out.

se the same technique to cover a journal or other book—just change the dimensions.

Slip your checkbook in its original plastic cover into the new T-shirt cover. Now, for that bill-paying party . . .

"[The T-shirt] is the only piece of clothing that adapts to your desires. It is at times an under-garment, at others an outer garment, and it changes with habits and seasons."

—designer Helmut Lang

a tee in the 'pod

I n the heavily anticipated reunion performance, T-shirts, together again with rock 'n' roll. Or . . . bluegrass, if that's your playlist. Turn up the volume while you work, and keep it up even after the project is made. Grab your scissors— Martha Stewart is about to meet digital entertainment and the DIY sparks will fly. (*Note:* These directions work for the dimensions of the iPod original model, so measure and alter your cozy accordingly.)

LEVEL 4

Lay the T-shirt flat and decide what part of it you'd like to have appear on the outside of the cozy (most likely a graphic from the front or back). From that area, cut two 3" by 4¼" rectangles (through both layers of fabric). Pin each of the double-layered rectangles together.

With your scissors, gently round off the corners of the rectangles, as shown.

---
ingredients
---

1 T-shirt
ruler
tailor's chalk
scissors
straight pins
needle
thread
1 punk pin

Sew around the edges of each pair of rectangles (completely sealing them) using an external whipstitch.

Pick your favorite punk pin and attach it to the center of the front of the pouch (opposite the strip, step 4), being sure to pin through only the first layer of the front panel. (If you go through both layers of fabric, you might scratch your screen.)

Cut a strip (about ½" by 8") from the rest of the T-shirt. Secure one end of the strip to the center of one of the sewn pairs (on the graphic side) using a single boxed cross-stitch.

Make your music selection, slip the player in, wrap the strip snugly around the pin, and plug in.

variations

Place the two sewn pairs together, graphic sides out. Sew the panels together on three sides (stopping ½" from the top edge, as shown), using a whipstitch.

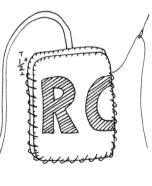

For a more visibly decorative look, use embroidery thread to stitch up the sides.

Make the pouch narrower (2½" by 4¼" rectangles), and you can stow a cell phone or mini iPod instead.

Make the pouch a little taller (2½" by 5¼"), and you can be oh-so-discreet with a tampon cozy.

i'm the real shady

If you peruse any of the sunglasses displays at mall kiosks, gas stations, or corner pharmacies, you'll notice that the shades not only offer 100% UV protection, but also come in an obscene number of styles and colors, too. For all the fashion-forward protection your shades give you, offer them swank asylum in your cozy T-shirt case in return.

LEVEL 2

Lay the T-shirt flat and mark and cut out a 3½" by 16" rectangle of fabric, through only one layer. Cut a ¾" by 18" strip from the bottom of the T-shirt to use as a drawstring.

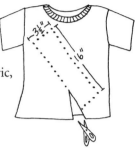

Fold the rectangle in half short side to short side, with right sides together. (You should have a 3½" by 8" rectangle.) Pin the 8" sides together and sew with a whipstitch. Remove pins.

Fold over the top edge of the bag ¾" to 1", pin, and sew with a whipstitch (forming a casing for the drawstring).

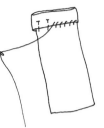

Turn the bag right side out. At the center top of the bag, about 1" apart, make two small vertical incisions through only one layer of fabric.

Thread the drawstring through one hole and out the other.

Slip your shades in, pull the drawstring, and drop them into your bag, scratch-free!

tee trivia

The 1950s greasers used the T-shirt as container—cigarette boxes rolled in their sleeves.

celebri-tee corner

The Tipping Point: A North Carolina elementary school got some unexpected attention from **Avril Lavigne** fans after the singer wore a vintage T-shirt bearing the school's name in her "Sk8er Boi" music video. The PTO received so many calls from people who wanted the tee that the green-and-gold number (right) was reprinted and sold, raising more than $25,000 for the school.

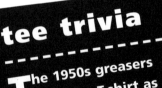

Handbags are perhaps the final word on female accessories. It is sometimes said that a woman's life is contained within its clutches, and when you think about what you stash in there on a Saturday night, it is true. Handbag designer Sylvia Venturini Fendi once said, "I obsess about the materials of the bag to the point of exhaustion." Well, no obsessing here—two T-shirts are all you need. It's light, soft, comfortable, and unfussy—it's cute, too, with a funky shape, subtle stitching, and a bow on top. (Just be on the lookout for younger sisters with sticky fingers, because this project *is* a one-size-fits-all.)

LEVEL 5

---
ingredients
---

2 T-shirts
(in different colors)

ruler

tailor's chalk

scissors

straight pins

needle

thread

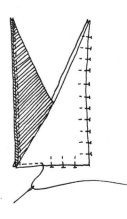

Lay both T-shirts flat. Measure, mark, and cut from each shirt vertical right triangles (through front and back layers) with dimensions of 9" by 23" by 25". (You'll have four triangles, two in each color.) *Note:* Use a paper pattern if you prefer.

Place two triangles of the same color against each other (right sides together) and pin and sew along the 23" edge. Repeat with the other two triangles.

Insert the tips of one pair of triangles between the layers of the other, so that the 9" sides completely overlap. Line up the 9" edges of all four layers and pin them. Sew along the pinned edges with a small, secure running backstitch. Remove pins.

(*Note:* The triangles that you insert will be the ones visible on the outside of the finished handbag, so arrange them accordingly.)

Turn the bag right side out. Pin the overlapping edges of fabric together, as shown. Sew the pinned edges using a whipstitch or running stitch, being careful to stitch together only two layers at a time (so you don't accidentally sew the bag closed!). Remove pins.

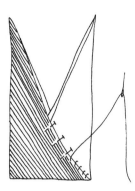

Tie the points at the top together in a double knot, leaving 2" tails. Slip in your wallet, keys, and cell phone, sling it over your shoulder, and go.

In 2004, shoe designer Farylrobin took the T-shirt to another level—the ground level. Decorated in vintage T-shirt fabric, these heels were made for rockin'.

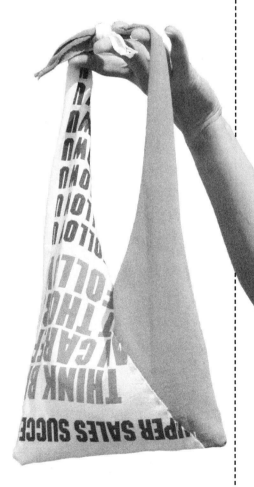

backpacking the heat

Backpacks usually remind me of summer's end and heading back to school. But made of T-shirts, this backpack holds sun-baked memories of beach days, road trips, and rock concerts. . . . This is a project that can be made with one T-shirt, but to make it really durable, use two. (Especially if you're using very old, very loved, very worn tees.)

LEVEL 4

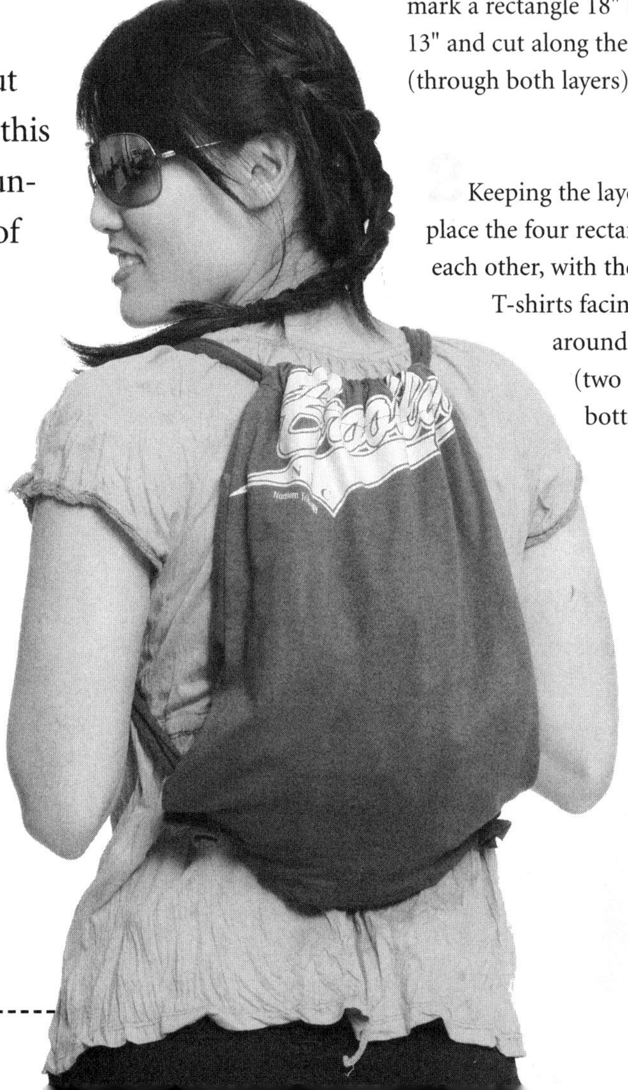

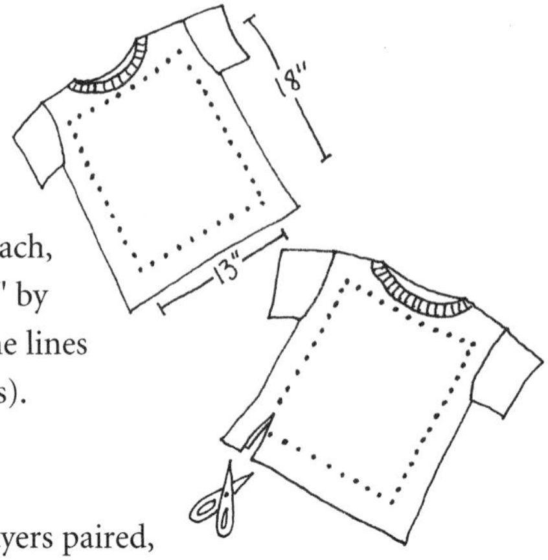

Lay both T-shirts flat. From each, mark a rectangle 18" by 13" and cut along the lines (through both layers).

Keeping the layers paired, place the four rectangles against each other, with the fronts of the T-shirts facing in. Pin around three edges (two sides and the bottom).

ingredients

2 T-shirts (M or L)
ruler
tailor's chalk
scissors
straight pins
needle
thread
seam ripper (optional)

Sew along the pinned edges using a tight whipstitch. Remove pins.

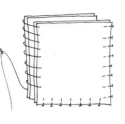

From the scrap pieces of one of the T-shirts, cut two strips 1¾" wide and 48" long (double the length of the T-shirt).

Fold over the top edge 1" all the way around the opening of the bag, and pin.

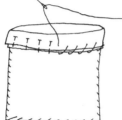

At each side of the drawstring casing, snip or seam-rip a ½"-long slit through only the top layer of fabric.

Sew the pinned edge down using a whipstitch. (This will be the casing for your drawstrings.) Remove the pins and turn the backpack right side out.

About 1" from each of the lower corners of the backpack, poke a small hole through all four layers.

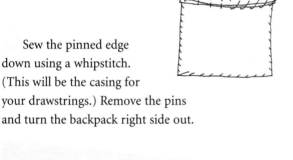

celebri-tee corner

The fifth time's the charm! Actress **Julia Stiles** slashed up five different T-shirts in order to get her self-styled halter just right for the MTV Movie Awards in 2001.

Thread one of the drawstrings through one of the slits you made in step 7, around the entire perimeter of the top of the backpack, and out the same slit.

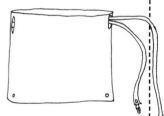

continued

10 Repeat step 9 with the second drawstring, threading it through the opposite slit. Pull both pairs of ends gently to make them even.

Thread two loose ends through a hole in the lower corner on the same side. Repeat on the other side. Tie the ends of each pair of strips in a knot to keep them from slipping out of the holes.

Fill up the backpack, pull the drawstrings closed, and sling it over your shoulders.

variation

ew pockets to the front, back, or inside of the backpack!

Some accessories have so defined the people or characters who wear them that the wearers and their signature accessories are inseparable. For example, if somebody says "white glove," Michael Jackson immediately comes to mind. Match the wearers below with their identifying accessories:

1. Luke Skywalker
2. Siegfried and Roy
3. Madonna
4. Linus
5. The Dude
6. Humphrey Bogart
7. Hester Prynne
8. King Arthur
9. Carmen Miranda
10. Groucho Marx
11. J-Lo
12. Frodo
13. Cinderella

A. fruit basket hat
B. Excalibur
C. glass slipper
D. The Ring
E. light saber
F. conical bra
G. white tigers
H. blanket
I. a White Russian
J. scarlet letter
K. cigar
L. fedora
M. rear end (once it's insured, it's an accessory)

(Answers: 1.E; 2.G; 3.F; 4.H; 5.I; 6.L; 7.J; 8.B; 9.A; 10.K; 11.M; 12.D; 13.C)

rock the tote

You could make this tote out of just one T-shirt, but to make it really functional—strong enough to hold the contents of your life—double the thickness. And this way, you'll have a somewhat reversible bag (not inside out, but backside front). Pair T-shirt opposites (black with white, pink with blue, a skull and crossbones with a Hello Kitty) and you'll be sporting a very Dr. Jekyll–Mr. Hyde look. **LEVEL 4**

Lay both T-shirts flat, cut off the hem, and cut a 5"-wide tube from the bottom of each shirt. Cut through one side of each tube to make two long strips. Trim the ends so that both strips are the same length and set them aside.

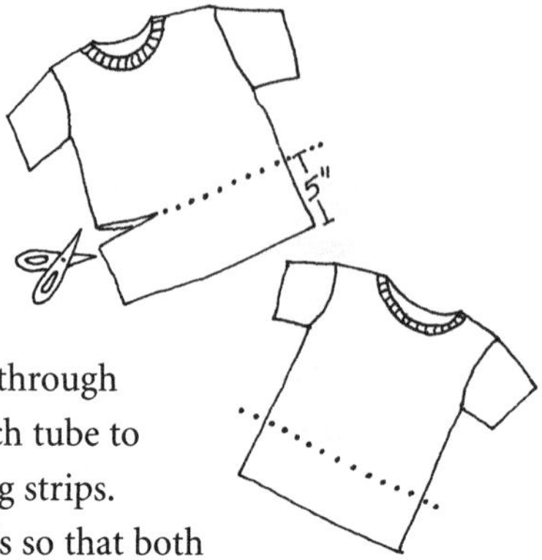

From both shirts, cut rectangles approximately 14" wide by 15" long through both layers. You should have two pairs of rectangles.

ingredients

- 2 T-shirts (M or L)
- ruler
- tailor's chalk
- scissors
- straight pins
- needle
- thread

Keeping the layers paired, place the four rectangles against each other, with the fronts of the T-shirts facing in. Pin along the long sides of the rectangles through all four layers.

Sew along the pinned edges using a whipstitch. Remove the pins.

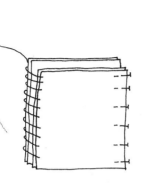

Take one of the strips (from step 1) and fold its edges ½" toward the center (making the strip 4" wide). Then fold the strip in half (creating a 2"-wide strip) and pin the edges. Repeat with the second strip.

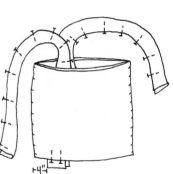

Pinch one end of strip #1 and one end of strip #2 together, and thread them through the rectangular tube from top to bottom. Allow the strips to stick out of the bottom about 1" and position them about 4" in from the side seam. Pin them in place.

continued

celebri-tee corner

In order to get out the young vote for the 2004 presidential election, rap mogul **Sean "Diddy" Combs** launched a T-shirt campaign, "Vote or Die!" His dramatic message was powered by such stars as Alicia Keys, Leonardo DiCaprio, Snoop Dogg, Paris Hilton, Mary J. Blige, Mariah Carey, and Usher.

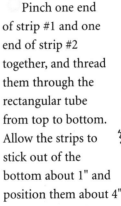

7 Without twisting the strips, pinch the other two ends together and repeat step 6, pinning them in place 4" from the other side seam.

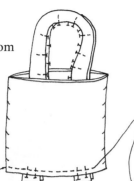

8 Sew across the bottom of the rectangle using a small running back-stitch, being sure to sew through all four layers of the rectangle as well as both layers of the straps. Remove the pins from the bottom of the rectangle. (Do not remove the pins along the straps.)

9 Fold the unsewn top edge of the rectangle down 1" and sew it in place, using a whipstitch. Turn the tote right side out.

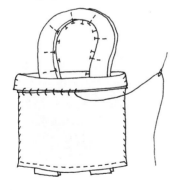

10 Starting at the bottom edge, pin the straps to the outside of the tote.

11 Sew along the edges of both strips using a running stitch, fastening them to their respective sides of the tote. Continue stitching along the handle edges. Remove all pins.

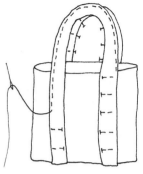

Optional: Reinforce the four intersections (where the handles meet the top of the tote) with a single boxed cross-stitch.

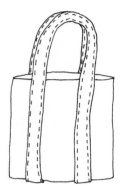

12 Load up and rock out.

variation

8 dd a pocket or two for extra storage (on the inside or outside). See project 16, Pocket It.

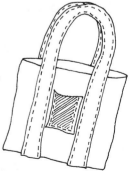

is this seat taken?

Your booty. You can shake it, park it, get it kicked, or get knocked flat on it. Try this project to cushion the blow. It's a trendy cosmopolitan alternative to the traditional country gingham. And let's face it, at the end of the day, you want to be able to put your feet up and give your backside a little stylish TLC.

ingredients

- 1 T-shirt (L or XL)
- ruler
- tailor's chalk
- scissors
- straight pins
- needle
- thread
- 1 bag of pillow stuffing
- 4 punk pins or buttons

Measure the length and width of the chair seat you want to pad and add 1" (x). (For example, if the chair seat is 16" by 16", your measurement will be 17" by 17".) Spread the T-shirt flat and mark and cut out a square from the center with those dimensions, being sure to cut through both layers of fabric.

continued

Gently round the edges on all four corners.

Cut two matching strips (1" wide by 24" long) from the remaining fabric of the T-shirt.

Fold one strip in half and pin the folded point to the right side of the fabric at the corner of one square, as shown. Do the same with the other strip, pinning it to a corner adjacent to the first.

Place the two squares, right sides together, and pin around the edges, tucking the strips inside.

Sew around the pinned perimeter ½" from the edge using a running backstitch (this will secure the strips, as well). (*Note:* Along the edge between the strips, leave 3" to 4" unsewn.)

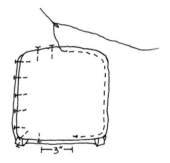

Remove the pins and turn the pouch you've created right side out through the opening.

tee trivia

Are you just another statistic? Of people 18 to 24 years old, 79% own more than 10 T-shirts—19% of that group have more than 30 T-shirts. What's in your closet?

8 Take some stuffing, pull it into smaller bits, and stuff it evenly throughout the cushion, until it reaches desired firmness.

11 Secure the cushion to your chair seat by tying the strips around the back frame of the chair, and take a load off.

9 Use a very small whipstitch to close up the 3" to 4" opening in the back of the cushion.

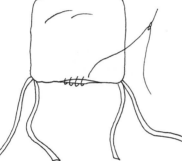

variations

Instead of the punk pins used in step 10, use embroidery thread and needle to make four stitches and knots.

10 Place the four punk pins in a square, pinning all the way through the cushion. (The pins keep the stuffing from migrating, and they look cool, too.)

Or, stitch on four buttons (sewing all the through the cushion) to replace the pins.

sweet dreams are made of tees

There's nothing softer than a pillow . . . well, maybe one thing—that worn-out T-shirt that's traveled everywhere with you. (Your mom won't let you wear it outside anymore, so you might as well put it to good use inside!) One of the easiest projects (c'mon, it's a rectangle), it's big on reward. When you finish, curl up and take a well-deserved nap. Just remember, the T-shirt you choose should be soft and dream-enhancing. (Only the hardcore can handle falling asleep on a skull and crossbones.)

LEVEL 3

Turn the T-shirt inside out, cut off the sleeves just inside the seams, and mark and cut a straight line across the shirt, just below the neck band. Cut off the bottom hem just above the stitching.

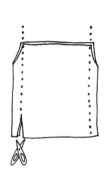

Starting at the top corners, mark straight lines parallel to the sides of the shirt. Cut along the lines (through both layers) to create a rectangle.

ingredients

1 T-shirt
ruler
tailor's chalk
scissors
needle
thread
1 bag of pillow stuffing (or a load of T-shirt scraps)

Sew the two panels together along all four sides using a running backstitch or whipstitch, leaving a 4" opening.

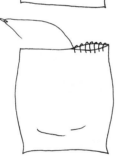

Turn the pillow right side out. Stuff it, pushing the stuffing into the corners of the pillow first.

variations

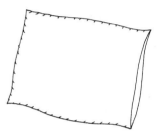

Once the pillow is filled to desired plumpness, sew the opening closed with a small, tight whipstitch.

f you're not ready to tackle the *whole* pillow, start with just the pillowcase—three straight lines of sewing and you're golden. Using a whipstitch, sew three sides of a rectangle, leaving what was the bottom edge of the T-shirt (already conveniently hemmed) untouched. Turn right side out and slide in a pillow! (Now wasn't that satisfying?)

ut more fabric off the top of the T-shirt to make a square throw pillow. Use a second T-shirt to make a contrasting backside to your pillow.

Haven't had time to launder the sheets? No problem. The original T-shirt pillowcase is ready-made—simply slip a pillow into a soft T-shirt, leaving those sleeves a-flappin' in the wind.

efore you sew the back and front panels together, attach a pocket. (Even if you have a full set of adult teeth, you can always hope the Tooth Fairy gets confused.)

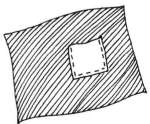

cute roll-up

For some reason, aerodynamically shaped objects are so much cooler. The Washington Monument? Much cooler than the Lincoln Memorial. The Corvette? Much cooler than the Town Car. The cheetah? Much cooler than the warthog. This streamlined, cute little pillow is no exception. Rock on with your big bad self. **LEVEL 3**

Follow steps 1 and 2 for the Sweet Dreams pillow (project 86).

Peel apart the two rectangles of fabric you're left with (A and B). Before setting aside one piece (A) for the cylindrical part of the pillow (the middle), measure the length of its longest side (x).

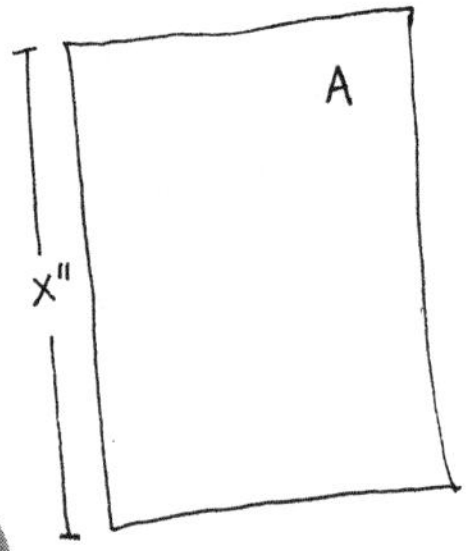

ingredients

- 1 T-shirt
- ruler
- tailor's chalk
- scissors
- straight pins
- needle
- thread
- T-shirt scraps or 1 bag of pillow stuffing

Fold the other piece of fabric (B), short end to short end, and lay it flat. Trace and cut a circle on B, making sure the circumference of the circle is equal to the measure of the longest side (X) of rectangular fabric A.

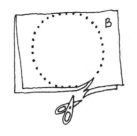

Take piece A and fold it in half, right sides in, matching short side to short side, and pin along that edge. Sew along the pinned edge using a whipstitch. Remove pins.

Place one circle piece at one open end of the cylinder piece (A) (right sides in) and pin the edges together. Repeat with the other circle piece on the other end of the cylinder. Sew along the pinned edges on both sides using a whipstitch, leaving a 2" opening on one end only.

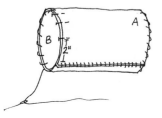

Go ahead and turn it right side out and stuff the pillow with your scraps. Once desired plumpness is reached, stitch the opening closed with a very small whipstitch.

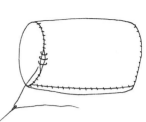

Prop it at your lower back or behind your neck and kick up your feet.

Optional: Use a second T-shirt in step 3 to provide contrasting end circles for the pillow.

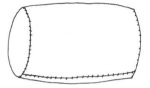

tees in the movies

Lost in Translation **(2003): "God, you *are* having a midlife crisis," says Charlotte (Scarlett Johannson) when Bob Harris (Bill Murray) shows up at her hotel room door wearing an orange camouflage T-shirt (that he promptly turns inside out).**

patchwork punk

Bar mitzvahs, sports teams, concerts, family vacations, and reunions—this project is for the really sentimental DIYer. You've saved not one or two T-shirts, but one or two *boxes* of T-shirts from those days of yore. You can't bear to let them go, but you know you'll never find use for that many Phish tour or basketball tournament T-shirts ever again. Here's the solution—a comfy, commemorative 7' by 7' patchwork blanket made of favorite T-shirts. It's the perfect keepsake—not to mention the perfect gift (for the college-bound kid or the happy couple's wedding). *Note:* You'll need a lot of floor space for this one, and if you have a sewing machine, use it to save time. **LEVEL 4**

Measure, mark, and cut 13" squares through both layers of each of the 25 T-shirts. (*Note:* You may choose to center the T-shirt design within each square or offset it to one side.)

---
ingredients
---

25 T-shirts

ruler

tailor's chalk

scissors

straight pins

needle

thread

1 flat sheet (king size)

embroidery needle

embroidery thread

Separate the pairs of squares and lay them out in a pattern seven squares wide by seven squares high. (*Note:* You'll have one square to spare— see variations.)

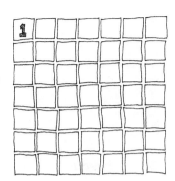

Starting at one corner of your layout, place two neighboring squares together, right sides in, and pin along their shared edge. About ½" in from the edge, sew along that pinned edge using a running backstitch. (If you open it up, you now have a 13" by 25" rectangle.)

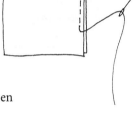

Remove the pins and repeat with the next neighboring square, working your way across the top row of your layout. Continue adding squares until you have seven in a horizontal sequence to complete the top row. (You will have a strip of "tiles" that measures approximately 13" by 85".)

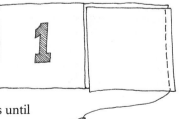

Start on the second row, using the same technique (steps 3 and 4) to sew together all the squares in that row.

Continue sewing together each horizontal row of squares, as above, until all seven rows have been completed.

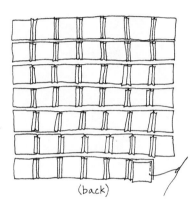

(back)

Place the adjoining edges of the top two rows together, right sides in, and pin them along that edge. Sew along the pinned edge ½" in from the edge. Remove pins.

Continue pinning and sewing together the adjoining edges of the remaining rows in the order in which you laid them out.

continued

Bar/bat mitzvah T-shirts have some of the tackiest slogans in the business . . . and that's why we love them so. Here's a Top 10 of T-shirts from those theme-inspired, coming-of-age, braces-wearing days:

BAR/BAT MITZVAH THEME	SLOGAN
10. *Star Wars*	"May the force be with you, Jonah."
9. Baseball	"I hit one out of the park at David's bar mitzvah!"
8. Late-night talk show	"Live from the Ed Sullivan Theater—Late Night with Elijah"
7. The Beatles	"Rebecca's Magical Mystery Tour: April 7, 1992"
6. Austin Powers	"Sarah's bat mitzvah was groovy, baby, very groovy."
5. Revolutionary War	"The British are coming! The British are coming! for Josh's bar mitzvah, 1986"
4. Olympics	"I went for the gold at Julie's bat mitzvah!"
3. Madonna	"I changed my name to Esther at Matthew's bar mitzvah!"
2. Magic	"Adam-cadabra!"
1. Endangered species/ *Moby Dick*	"I had a WHALE of a time at Sharon's bat mitzvah!"

9 Once you've completed the entire front panel, center it on top of the king-size flat sheet, right sides in, and pin around the edges. *Optional:* Add batting to the inside of the T-shirt layer to turn your blanket into a quilt.

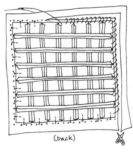

(back)

10 Trim the edges of the sheet so it is the same size as the T-shirt panel and, except for the width of one square at the bottom edge, sew around the pinned perimeter of the blanket (with a backstitch or whipstitch), ½" from the edge.

(back)

11 Turn the blanket right side out through the open square and stitch up the opening with a small whipstitch.

12 Using the embroidery needle and thread, at each intersection of squares attach the top and bottom layers by making a single down-up stitch. Tie off the thread ends in a square knot, leaving about 1" dangling.

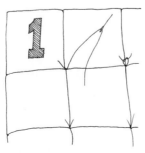

13 Snuggle up!

variations

pare a square: Use the square you set aside in step 2 to appliqué a shape onto one of the other squares. (Or add a pocket to a quilt square for a secret message.)

on't sew the bottom seam completely (leave the length of three squares open) to make a groovy duvet cover. It's the domestic diva's dream—so easy to wash!

peaking of domestic: Use the individual squares to make a set of cloth napkins. Or sew fewer squares together to make a checkered tablecloth.

ake a set of window drapes using only six T-shirts (front and back) but a similar patching technique. Stitch together two mini "blankets," each about 24" by 48" (two 12" panels wide by four 12" panels high). Sew four reinforced loops at the top of each curtain (to fit a dowel through), and hang.

chapter 7

trash talk

After the T-shirt deconstruction and reconstruction, here are 19 projects for assessing the impact zone. Use the scraps (or "wreckage") to make small accessories, like earrings, flower blossoms, and wristbrands, or turn a whole pile of scraps into a shag or spiral rug. Get scrappy with already existing garments by adding pockets or "wedges."

Along with trashed hotel rooms, wrecked T-shirts are enduringly linked with rock 'n' roll. At the end of your Tee Party, after you've slashed and shredded to your heart's content and rocked till the break of dawn, you may find yourself with a bit of a mess to clean up, too. T-wrecks (a.k.a. the T-shirt scraps) are the ultimate challenge once you've already recycled the tee and remade it as saucy, punk, or glam. So, what *do* you do with the dregs—the leftovers gathered around your feet? Get scrappy. This is a lesson in picking up the pieces.

Think of it this way. Cover bands often get a bum rap, accused of being unoriginal. But there are a few true artists among them who are hailed as recycling gods; rather than dirtying up the sound waves with sonic debris, they breathe new life into old classics. Sinead O'Connor covered Prince's "Nothing Compares 2 U" with astounding success. And Bob Dylan's "All Along the Watchtower" covered by Jimi Hendrix, with its unforgettable guitar riffs, is revered as genius. You get the idea. They took something originally by someone else, transformed it, and made it theirs. But even more appropriate to the T-wrecks model are the rap and hip-hop artists who sample just a piece—a chorus, a line, a hook—from an oldies song and attach it to an original beat.

Honoring that same tradition, use every last bit of the T-shirt to make some of your most original masterpieces yet—

accessories that interpret the shape of the T-shirt so loosely that the folks at Fruit of the Loom could never have imagined them as they pieced together the original tee. Superhero wrist cuffs, a ring, a shag rug? To the rallying cry of "mend it, don't end it," wave your flag—uh, how about a T-shirt?—high and challenge yourself. Throw none of it away. Think of this as recycling, composting, or the ultimate clean plate club. . . . Dig in.

flower power

There are a number of ways to render flowers from fabric—from a very provocative open blossom to a demure rosebud. And you can put them anywhere —at the base of a skirt, at its waist, at the neckline of a shirt, on the bodice of a tank top. Two well-placed flowers applied to the bikini top will make a perfect set of pasties. Or, pin them like a brooch on a hat or a blazer lapel. **LEVEL 3**

Lay the T-shirt sleeve flat and mark and cut (through both layers) a rectangle 3½" by 1¾".

tee trivia

It takes about six miles of yarn to make one T-shirt. (Think of that when you're about to throw those scraps away.)

ingredients

1 T-shirt sleeve
ruler
tailor's chalk
scissors
needle
thread

Use one rectangle as a pattern to cut a third identical rectangle from the rest of the sleeve.

Layer all three rectangles on top of each other and, with your scissors, round off the corners to make a pill-shape.

Separate the three pill-shaped pieces and sew right down the center of each piece using a basting stitch, as shown. Pull the hanging thread ends together, gathering the fabric in the center, and tie the ends of your thread (creating a peanut or hourglass shape).

Layer the three pieces on top of each other, rotating each slightly, so that they splay out like a fan (and will look like petals of a flower). For a more full-figured flower, double the recipe and use six pill-shaped pieces.

Pinch the petals together between your thumb and forefinger. Inserting your needle from the back to the front, sew the fabric layers in petal formation using a running stitch. (You may sew in a circle for a decorative flower center, but more haphazard stitches are fine, since they'll be hidden in the gathers.)

Now sew or pin the flower to one of your leg warmers or gauntlets, or attach it to a hair ribbon for flowers in your hair!

variations

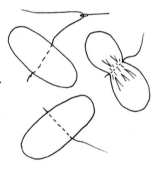

or a **no sew** version, pin all the splayed-out petal layers together in the middle from the back with a safety pin and attach a round punk pin to the front as the flower's center.

nip it in the bud

A *rose is a rose is a rose.* Until it's made from a T-shirt. Resistant to wilting and fading, no thorns, no aphids—this one's got staying power. **LEVEL 3**

ingredients

1 T-shirt sleeve
ruler
tailor's chalk
scissors
needle
thread

From a T-shirt sleeve, measure and cut one 7" by 2" strip. Fold the strip of fabric in half lengthwise, creating a new 7" by 1" double-thick strip. Sew along the open length of the strip using a basting stitch.

Gather the fabric over the thread, as shown. Secure the gathers by backstitching over the last few basting stitches.

Starting at one end, gently roll up the strip and pinch the base (the edge with stitching) together. Sew in and out through the pinched end to secure the roll in place.

Attach to a garment or accessory, and wear proudly.

variation

ake a handful of rosebuds and stick them on chopsticks (stems) for a witty bouquet that will never wilt.

ice t

This is the un-bling ring. It's the "ice" of T-shirt jewelry. The tiny decorative stitches are like small diamonds encircling the band. **LEVEL 3**

ingredients

1 small T-shirt scrap

ruler

tailor's chalk

scissors

straight pins

needle

thread

From a scrap, measure and cut a rectangle 1¾" wide by 3" long. With the wrong side up, fold one of the long sides two thirds of the way to the other side.

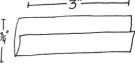

Fold the other side down over the first folded edge and pin. Sew down the center of the strip using a small running stitch.

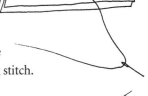

Sew two more lines of running stitches along either side of the first line.

Fold the strip in half (right sides in) and pin along the short edges. Try on and adjust the size to fit. Sew, using a running backstitch or a whipstitch along the pinned edges.

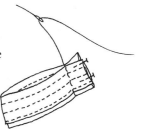

Turn it right side out, trim excess fabric, and slip it on.

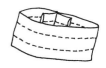

banned for life

You can cut the neckpiece out of a T-shirt and slip it over your head as an instant headband, or you can take a few more steps for a more glamorous payoff. There are a number of ways to style this one, so be creative: Wrap it, twist it, tie it, or knot it. Test its multipurpose potential by trying it as a belt or a hatband.

LEVEL 3

1. Lay the two tubes flat next to each other and snip through the sides of each tube to make approximately 48"-long strips.

---

ingredients

- 2 tubes (2" to 3") from the bottoms of 2 T-shirts (in different colors)
- ruler
- scissors
- straight pins
- needle
- thread

2   Lay the strips on top of each other, right sides together, and pin them along both edges. Trim at one end so that they're the same length.

3   Using a whipstitch, sew the two strips together along the pinned edges (leaving the ends open). Remove the pins and turn the band right side out.

4   Press the band flat so that the seam is in the center, splitting the two colors like a black-and-white cookie.

5   Wrap the band around your head so that the ends are at the top of your forehead. Tie them in a single knot.

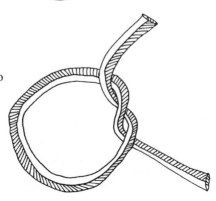

6   Twist the two ends together to form a single rope, and spiral the rope around the knot so that it fits tightly against your head. It'll look a bit like a flower.

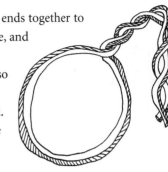

7   Secure the end by tucking it in between wraps in the spiral. Adjust the band so that the "flower" rests slightly to one side. (*Note:* This wrap is temporary. If you want the spiral to last, slip the band gently off your head and stitch the knot in place.)

variation

For a **no sew** (and spiral-free) head wrap, take the bottom loop off a T-shirt (a tube 4" to 5" wide), loop it once to double it, and slide it around your head, pulling the hair back from your face.

net profits

Make no mistake, this is *not* your lunch lady's hairnet. In fact, it can be a rather elegant way of containing your tangle of hair. . . . Just note, all you short-haired ladies, that this one does require that you *have* a tangle of hair. Otherwise, you'll end up with the equivalent of a bizarre-looking yarmulke. **LEVEL 2**

1 Fold the 7" by 7" square in half and mark and cut a half-circle from the folded edge. (Unfold it and you should have a circle.)

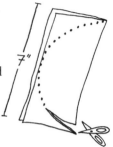

2 Starting at the center of the circle, draw concentric circles about ½" apart, stopping at least 1" from the edge.

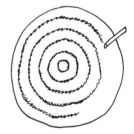

ingredients

- 1 T-shirt scrap, 7" by 7"
- tailor's chalk
- ruler
- scissors or razor blade
- 1 T-shirt scrap strip, 1" by 12"

Along each of the circular lines, make 1½" cuts ½" apart with your scissors or razor, creating netting, as shown. On the outermost ring (1" from the edge), make an even number of cuts ½" long and ½" apart. (*Note:* If you use a razor, make sure that you have a cutting mat or a piece of scrap cardboard to place underneath the fabric.)

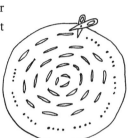

Use the T-shirt strip as a drawstring, weaving it in and out of the outermost ring of slits.

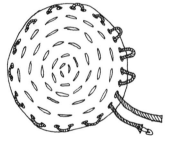

Wrap your hair into a bun and catch any stray wispies by placing the net over it, pulling the drawstrings into a tight bow.

variation

or another **no sew** project, score a hole in one with a set of golf club covers. Simply follow steps 1, 3, and 4 above, and you're ready to tee off. For the full set: You could make a matching set out of one T-shirt, or use a number of smaller multicolored scraps to add a splash of rainbow to the green.

tee trivia

Causin' Trouble: An FAA investigation ensued in 1998 when a group of teenagers celebrating their graduation held a wet T-shirt contest in the cockpit of a Boeing 727 during their flight to Mexico.

i'm with the band

Zorro has his mask, Superman has his cape, Wonder Woman has her Golden Lasso of Truth. Now you can have wristbands that embrace that whole bit, transforming any outfit to superhero status. It's a great gift or party favor.

LEVEL 3

ingredients

- 2 large T-shirt sleeves
- ruler
- tailor's chalk
- scissors
- 1 T-shirt sleeve in a different color
- needle
- thread
- straight pins

1 Lay the two shirt sleeves flat, cut them open along the seam, cut off the hems, and then cut two 2" by 14" rectangles from each sleeve.

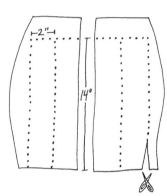

2 Pair off the strips and lay them on top of each other, wrong sides together. Mark and trim the corners so that each strip comes to a point at both ends (for tying).

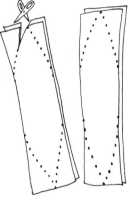

3 From the third T-shirt sleeve, draw and cut out two five-pointed stars, measuring about 2" from point to point.

Separate two of the strips and lay them right side up. Place one star in the middle of each strip and pin it in the center. Using a running stitch, appliqué the stars in place.

Now pin the top layers (with the stars) to the bottom strips (sans stars), wrong sides together.

Sew around the edges of the wristbands using a whipstitch. (*Note:* If you're lucky enough to be using a sewing machine, use a zigzag stitch around the perimeter, which allows stretch around the wrist.)

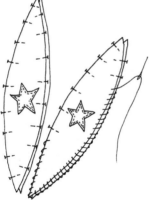

Remove all pins and tie them on.

(back)

variations

try appliquéing other shapes: a spiral, a dot, your initials (one on each wrist), a heart, or an "X marks the spot."

make your wristbands opposites: one is black with a yellow star; the other yellow with a black star.

Or, skip the fabric shape altogether, grab a handful of small gold safety pins, and arrange them in the shape of a sunburst.

my ears are ringing

T hough they're coming from the scrap heap, these earrings actually have the potential to look very glamorous. And hey, funky and functional, too— fold the end up into your ear and they act as earplugs.

LEVEL 2

ingredients

T-shirt scraps
ruler
tailor's chalk
scissors
1 paper clip
1 pair French hook earring backs
needle-nose pliers

Cut two 2" squares from one scrap and two 2" squares from another (two different colors).

Lay out the squares so the grains of the fabric (the direction of the stitches) all run in the same direction. This will ensure that the squares curl the same way. Bend out one end of the paper clip and use it to poke a *small* hole in the top corner of each of the four squares, about ⅛" from the edge.

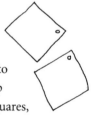

Use the pliers to very slightly bend open the hook of one earring back.

4 Slip one square of each color, right sides facing each other onto the hook. Close the hook back up with the pliers.

5 Repeat steps 3 and 4 for the second earring, and try on.

tees in the movies

Singles (1992): Kyra Sedgwick, as Linda Powell, illustrates the classic cleansing act of using the ex-boyfriend's intentionally "left behind T-shirt" to scrub the toilet.

variations

1 Layer two pieces of fabric, one slightly smaller than the other, for a study in color theory à la Josef Albers.

2 Try different shapes and see how they curl.

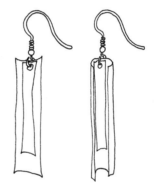

3 Although this is a no-sew project, you can make the earrings more secure by reinforcing the holes by stitching around them.

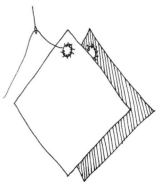

downward spiral

I t takes quite a few scraps to get a substantial rug, so either save up scraps for a while or be ready to donate quite a few T-shirts to the cause. The braiding and stitching process is very therapeutic (or maybe the spiraling motion is just hypnotic), and it's something you can do while watching TV or talking on the phone. This project is labeled a Level 4 not because of difficulty, but because of the time it requires—let's just say it's not going to be an afternoon.

LEVEL 4

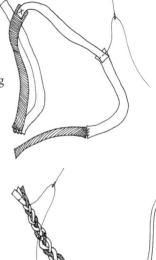

1 Cut scraps into strips 1" to 1½" wide. Sew them end to end using a whipstitch, a running backstitch, or a cross-stitch.

2 Sew three ends of the long strips together, and braid them. Keep adding strips and braiding them until you have the desired length. (*Note:* You'll need about 1,050" of braiding— or 87½'—to make a rug approximately 30" in diameter.)

---
ingredients

- strips of T-shirts (dozens, depending on length)
- scissors
- needle
- thread

3 Making sure the braid is lying flat, start the spiral by folding about 2" of the braid against itself. Sew the two braided edges together using a whipstitch on the bottom of the rug.

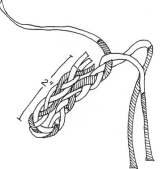

4 Keep spiraling the braid, sewing it to the base of the rug as you go. (*Note:* It's a good idea to stop about every 24" inches of braid and press the rug out on the floor to make sure you're not spiraling too tight—otherwise the rug will curl and buckle.)

5 When you've reached the desired size, snip any excess ends, sew the three strips together, and stitch them against the side of the rug.

variations

If you want to bail on the time commitment for the full rug, stop after you get to 8" in diameter for a braided spiral hot pad.

Make it a little bit bigger (about 10" to 12" in diameter), and you've got a stool cushion. *Optional:* Add four pairs of strips spaced evenly around the perimeter to tie the cushion to the top of each stool leg.

Or, make it even smaller (using strips ½" to ¾" wide) and weave a set of Rockin' Roller Coasters.

shag me, baby

If the spiral rug isn't your bag, baby, maybe a magnificently shag-a-delic rug is. It's the perfect addition to a lioness's lair. After all, we need something to knead our claws into from time to time. **LEVEL 3**

Lay the T-shirt flat and cut a rectangle approximately 24" by 18" from one layer.

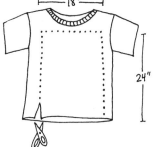

Starting 1" in from the edges, take the rectangle, and mark and carefully poke (or snip) horizontal and vertical rows of small holes about ½" to ⅔" apart.

ingredients

1 T-shirt (XL)

ruler

tailor's chalk

scissors

lots of small T-shirt scraps (cut into strips 5" to 6" long and 1" to 1½" wide)

safety pin

3 Attach a safety pin to one end of a strip and thread it down through the first hole, leaving a 2" tail. Pull it back up through the second hole.

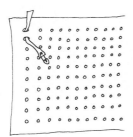

4 With the next strip, thread it down through the second hole (the same hole you just pulled the first strip through) and up through the third. The following strip goes down through the third hole and up through the fourth, and so on. (*Note:* If you have long strips, keep threading them up and down, leaving 2"-long loops instead of tails. Then snip through the top of the loops to create the 2" long shag.)

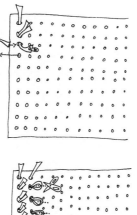

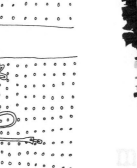

5 As the finishing touch, give your shag a little haircut if the ends need to be evened out (or unevened). Just know that it won't grow back, so yes, a buzz cut will undo hours of work.

variations

Once you get the hang of the technique, try some different designs—make stripes of color across the rectangle, concentric rectangles, or color blocks.

You'll notice that the pattern of your "stitches" on the underside of the rug (left) has a completely different but awesome woven look, so feel free to flip the rug over if the mood strikes you.

Make two square rugs, sew them together, and stuff them to make a magnificently cuddly, long-haired pillow.

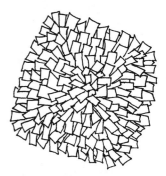

get scrappy

Some projects are more about the application of an already existing scrap than about making something completely new. Here's a collection of ideas for using T-shirts strips of varying length. Almost all of them are **no sew**. We like that.

big hair bands

take any strip at least ¾" wide (no more than 2") to make elastic bands for your hair. Without twisting the strip, stitch the ends securely together. (*Note:* Cut a ¾"-wide loop all the way around a scrap sleeve, and the project becomes **no sew**.) Gently tug the loop to make the edges curl. Wrap it (as many times as necessary) around a clump of hair, and layer a number of multicolored strips down your ponytail for a rainbow effect.

the bowed and the beautiful

hair ribbons are perhaps the easiest use for scraps—no extra cutting or sewing involved. You just need to be able to wrap the scrap around the end of your braid, your pigtail, or the small spikes of hair you've arranged all over your head, allowing sufficient length to tie a bow. You can twist several strips together before tying them for a multicolored look.

With any extras, decorate the buttonholes of your tattered jean jacket by threading a scrap strip through the hole and tying it.

brace yourself

this is a very simple project I made one afternoon after school at a friend's house. It's an accessory I wore for the rest of the year and have held onto ever since, stashing it in a small

pouch in the secret compartment of my jewelry box—along with a four-leaf clover and a heart locket that used to be my mom's.

All you need to do is cut a 1"-wide strip just above the bottom hem (or the end of one of the shirtsleeves) about 1" longer than the circumference of your wrist. You can just tie it on, but the original was clasped with a single gold safety pin at the 1" overlap. I decorated the bracelet with a peace sign (using a permanent silver marker), but you can leave it plain and let the colors do the talking. Another alternative: Replace the safety pin with a punk pin, or add many punk pins like trinkets on a charm bracelet.

102 knit wit

f you do the knitting thing, try this on for size: Sew the strips together as if you were making the Downward Spiral braided rug (project 96), and wind the resulting single "yarn" into a ball. Grab your extra-large needles (or use two turkey basters), cast on, and knit a scarf (above), a headband, or a belt.

101 lace station

ou'll need T-shirt strips at least 48" long (¾" to 1" wide) for a pair of sneakers, or be willing to stitch enough strips tightly together to make them long enough to add colorful T-shirt sentimentality to your Doc Martens. Simply lace 'em up and pull 'em tight. Of course, if the shoes you have in mind call for shorter laces, it'll be that much easier to find strips that fit the bill. (*Hint:* If getting the strips through the eyelets is really testing your patience, wrap tape around the tips to make threading easier.)

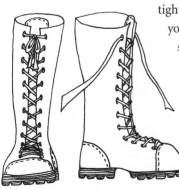

the it doll

This one is a shout-out to my best friend in junior high. She and I made at least five of these dolls (from her mom's pile of T-shirt scraps) and planned to market them as the "It Doll"—the doll that was neither male nor female, black nor white—before we figured out that It wouldn't pay our college tuition. So let me try to pitch it again: The It Doll can be pulled, pinched, punched, balled up, and launched. It's the sock monkey of the new millennium. And softer than your teddy bear. Oh, and use it as a pin cushion, and you've got yourself a voodoo doll. All for the bargain price of . . . FREE! **LEVEL 4**

Turn the T-shirt tube inside out and lay it flat. Use chalk to draw or trace the shape of your doll on the top layer of the T-shirt tube (approximately 5" by 20"); see illustration.

Cut around the lines you drew, through both layers of fabric.

----
ingredients
----

1 bottom tube of a T-shirt, 5" wide

tailor's chalk

scissors

straight pins

needle

thread

1 bag of stuffing or T-shirt scraps

3   Stack the two pieces on top of each other, wrong sides in, matching up the edges and pinning them together.

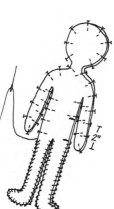

4   Starting at one side of the torso (think appendix region), sew along the perimeter of the doll using a whipstitch. Leave a 2" opening.

5   Keep your needle and thread attached and stuff the doll through the opening in its side, pushing small bits into the extremities first.

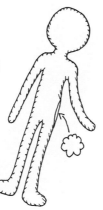

6   Once the doll has reached desired plumpness, stitch up the opening using a whipstitch and tie it off.

7   Take a bow.

variations

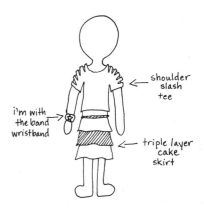

If you want to give your doll more of an identity, place two punk pins on the face as eyes (kind of alien-esque).

Or, toss gender neutrality aside and place the pins slightly farther south to give your doll breasts!

Make a "Mini It" from smaller scraps (3" by 8").

Make any of the projects in this book on a smaller scale, and your doll's got an outfit for every day of the week.

shoulder slash tee

i'm with the band wristband

triple layer cake skirt

get snippy

By now you know that almost any scrap can be salvaged. Here are some projects that apply the T-shirt (or T-shirt scraps) to already existing pieces of clothing, for a hybrid result.

expand-o-pants

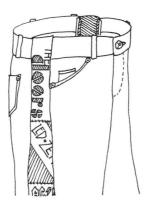

I went through a huge growth spurt in high school (meaning I not only got taller, but also wider), effecting a major wardrobe shift—after all, I had to find new clothes to fit my new body. Though I was thrilled to go on a shopping spree, I lamented the loss of some of my favorites (like the pair of Levi 501s I had begged my mom to buy me just two months earlier) to the giveaway pile. And so, I created a solution: "Expand-O-Pants." (Perfect for holiday overeating, bloating, birthdays, and bat mitzvahs.) Cut along both outside seams of a pair of pants (through the waistband). Sew T-shirt squares together into two long matching strips (you choose the width) and then sew them into the open side seams using a running or whipstitch. Ta-da! Newly expanded duds.

pocket it

Add a pocket to anything, and it's like you're adding a new handbag to your collection. And don't forget the endless "Is that a banana in your pocket . . . ?" jokes. One hour of sewing for unlimited hours of fun. Take the seam ripper to the rear of those jeans and remove one or both of the patch pockets. Use it as a pattern to cut matching pockets out of a T-shirt scrap and sew the new tee pockets in place of the old.

tee trivia

Did you know? Hard rockers go for soft T-shirts: Of all musical trends, the hard rock population has produced the largest group of T-shirt lovers.

106 patch it

(back)

Perhaps the easiest and most common project is the T-shirt patch. Keep it in mind for when that old Ramones T-shirt (hypothetically) is so threadbare that it looks like you're winning the wet T-shirt contest even on the driest of days. It's a way to preserve the spirit of a T-shirt having such sentimental value that you've gone to the trouble of coloring in the fading red R-A-M-O-N-E-S letters (hypothetically) with fabric paint every two years. I mean, come on, it was (hypothetically) your first rock 'n' roll T-shirt ever. Make it live on.

Cut out a square from your beloved T-shirt and use safety pins (or a needle and thread) to attach the patch to the back of your favorite jean jacket or hooded sweatshirt . . . or backpack or tote or even another T-shirt.

107 flare affair

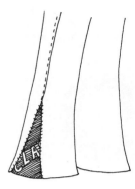

When punk goes hippie: Channel the late '60s with bell-bottoms made from trashed T-shirts. A style originally designed for function (Navy uniforms), bell-bottom pants hit the fashion scene with the likes of music legends James Brown and Elvis Presley. Grab your seam ripper and get ready to get up, get on up.

Seam-rip 10" up from the bottom of the outside of each pant leg. Sew a triangle wedge of T-shirt fabric into the gap in each leg. If you prefer a less conspicuous wedge, insert it in the inside pant leg seam. Or, if you want to double your pleasure, insert wedges in both the inside and outside pant leg seams.

tees in the movies

***Dream a Little Dream* (1989), Take 2: The back of Dinger's (Corey Haim's) signature sweatshirt is none other than a DIY patch job.**

tying the knot

Donna Karan, Marc Jacobs, Calvin Klein, Vera Wang. It's a long-standing tradition for a designer to cap a season's runway show with a wedding gown. This line from *Generation T* is no exception. It's your opportunity to get the perfect start on the *ultimate* budget wedding. A $4,000 wedding dress? Bah! Try well under $40. Here's the one occasion to go all out with your stylistic expression without going overboard on your budget. Something old, something new . . .

LEVEL 4

----
ingredients
----

7 white (or white with pattern) T-shirts (or 3 triple packs of large-size white T-shirts for a bright white)

ruler

tailor's chalk

scissors

straight pins

needle

thread

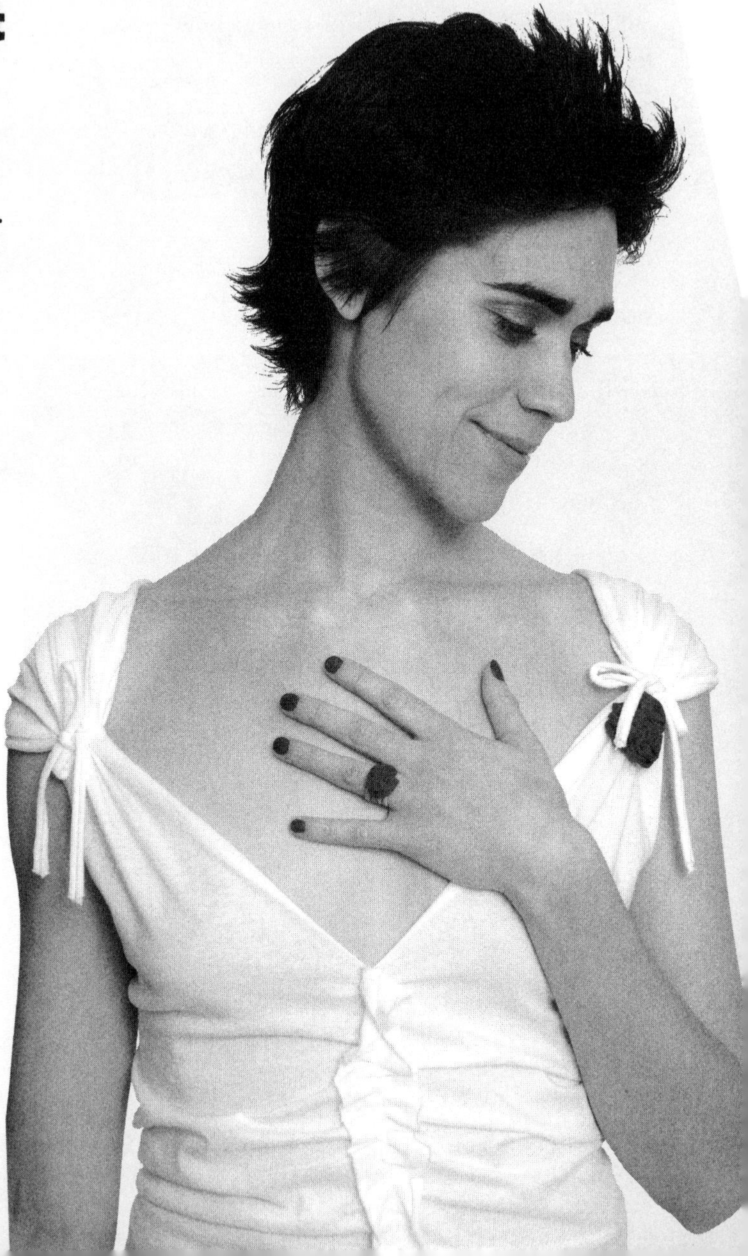

the top

This top is designed specifically to accompany the wedding skirt (with very little sewing), but if you prefer another look, it can be replaced by any of the tanks, tubes, or halters in Chapters 3 and 4.

Lay a white T-shirt flat and cut off the hem (save it to use in step 12 of the skirt). Cut off only the ends of the sleeves (just above the hem). Cut an additional 2" loop off the bottom of the shirt and set it aside.

Measure 10" down the front of the shirt starting at the neck band, mark it with a pin, and cut a slit, as shown.

Mark a straight line from the bottom of the slit to the bottom of the shirt. Measure that line (x), then cut a strip from the loop cut in step 1 that measures x long by 2" wide. (Save the remaining fabric for step 7.) Center and pin the strip over the chalk line, with both right sides up. Baste along the center of the strip through both layers. Remove pins.

Pull the thread and push against the fabric to gather the front of the shirt into a slight ruffle. (This will shorten the length from 14" to about 8".) Sewing along the same line, backstitch it in place.

Tuck the corners of the neck band inside the shirt to create a deep V-neck. Cut through the sleeve ends (from step 1) to make two 1"-wide strips. Cut off the hem stitching from their edges and tie them in bows around the front of the shoulders, bunching the sleeves.

Turn shirt over, mark the center back from the neck band to the hem edge. Cut along that line *only* through the back.

(back)

Cut the remainder of the 2" strip in half lengthwise (stretch it so you have two 1"-wide by 34"-long strips). Thread one strip through each armhole, wrap each end once around the sleeve (gathering it in the back), and tie the ends in a bow across the back of the shirt.

continued (back)

8 Twist the two cut edges to the inside and tie the corners together in a knot at the waist.

(back)

9 For a better fitting bodice, poke two small holes 1" in from the two twisted edges on the back and about 5" below the strip you tied in step 7. Thread the remaining 1" strip through the holes, wrap each end once around the twist, send it through the hole again, and tie it in the back.

10 Untie the bottom knot in the back, put the top on, retie the knot, and adjust the gathered cap sleeves over your shoulders as desired. Da-dum dedum, da-dum dedum . . .

the skirt:

1 Lay your six T-shirts flat and, one at a time, cut (through both layers) across the torsos just below the sleeves (creating tubes about 18" high).

2 Cut through one side of four of the resulting tubes to make four rectangles (each about 18" by 45").

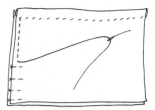

3 Place two of those rectangles together (wrong sides in), lining up the hemmed edges, and pin along one 18" edge. Sew ¼" in along the pinned edge using a backstitch, stopping at the hem stitching. (This creates a decorative external seam.) Repeat with the other two rectangles and remove all pins.

4 Take one of the two newly sewn rectangles and, with wrong sides together, pin one of the 18" edges to an 18" folded edge of one of the uncut tubes (from step 1). Pin the other edge of the rectangle to the other side of the tube, creating a much larger tube. Sew along both pinned edges ¼" from the edge using a backstitch and stopping at the hem. (The double-thickness tube becomes the front panel of the skirt.) Remove pins.

5 Repeat step 4 with the remaining rectangle and tube.

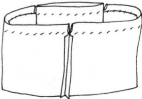

continued

tee trivia

Thirty-four percent of T-shirt wearers say white is the color of their favorite T-shirt.

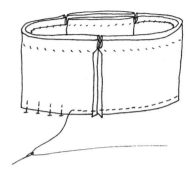

6 Insert one large tube inside the other, wrong sides together. Line up the double-layer panels and the hemmed edges. Pin the rough edges of the tubes together and sew ¼" from the edge using a backstitch.

7 From the tops of the six T-shirts, cut rectangles about 8" by 20" through both layers of fabric (cutting just inside the sleeves and just below the neckline).

8 Pin all the rectangles together along the 8" edges, wrong sides together, and sew ¼" from the edges using a backstitch, creating a wide loop.

9 Measure 1" down from the top edge of the loop and baste around the circumference of the entire loop.

10 Pull the thread and push the fabric to gather the ruffle so that each 20"-long panel is reduced to about 7" or 8" long.

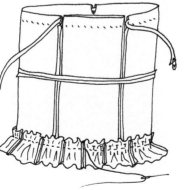

11 With the right sides facing up, pin the gathered ruffle around the bottom of the tube from step 6, placing the basting stitch line over the hem stitching. Adjust the gathers to fit the circumference of the skirt and sew over the basting stitch with a backstitch. Remove pins.

12 Cut off the bottom hem of a seventh T-shirt just below the hem stitching. Thread it through the drawstring casing of the two back panels at the top of the skirt. Pull the drawstring tight, gathering the back of the waistband into a small keyhole, and tie a bow. (A booty-shakin' bustle!) *Optional:* Add small tee rosebuds sprinkled around the skirt.

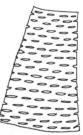

(back)

variations

For the full package, make a veil, bouquet, and ring. For the veil, cut a long trapezoid from a T-shirt and snip horizontal cuts into it using the mesh technique in project 27. For the bouquet, use chopsticks as stems and attach rosebuds (project 90). And seal the deal with the ring (project 91)!

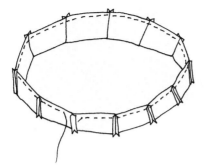

You don't have to stick with white—make it red hot, baby blue, or mellow yellow for prom night. Even a single panel of color gathered into the folds in the back of the skirt can make the dress a little more nontraditional.

do it yourself:

Sketch your own ideas for DIY T-shirt fashion here. Draw inspiration from streetwise pedestrians, music videos, mail-order catalogs, or store window displays . . . really, anywhere. Then grab a pair of scissors, because you could *so* make that.

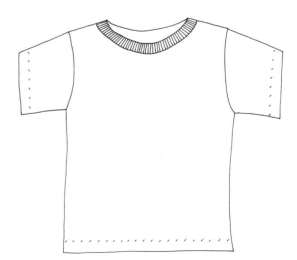

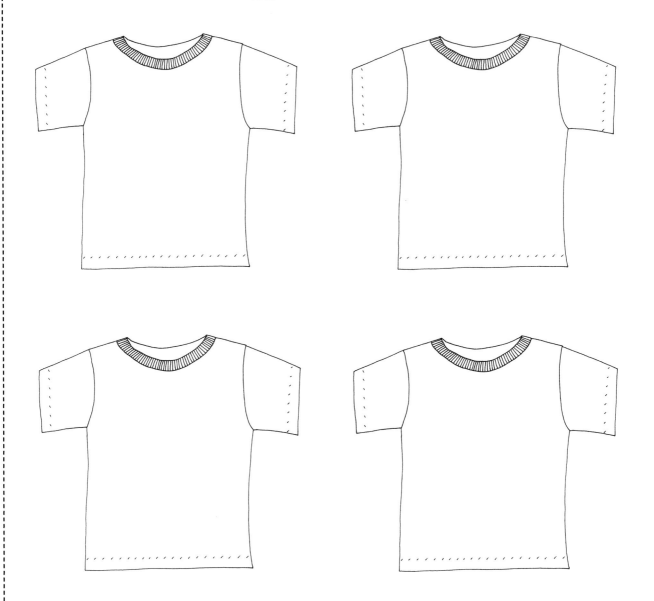

credits

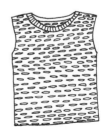
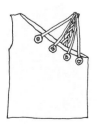